Also by Götz Aly

Hitler's Beneficiaries:
Plunder, Racial War, and the Nazi Welfare State

Architects of Annihilation:
Auschwitz and the Logic of Destruction
(with Susanne Heim)

Into the Tunnel

Into the Tunnel

The Brief Life of
Marion Samuel,
1931-1943

Götz Aly

TRANSLATED BY
ANN MILLIN

METROPOLITAN BOOKS
HENRY HOLT AND COMPANY
NEW YORK

Published in Association with the
United States Holocaust Memorial Museum

Metropolitan Books
Henry Holt and Company, LLC
Publishers since 1866
175 Fifth Avenue
New York, New York 10010
www.henryholt.com

Metropolitan Books® and ® are registered trademarks of Henry Holt and Company, LLC.

Originally published in Germany in 2004 under the title *Im Tunnel*
by S. Fischer Verlag, Frankfurt am Main.

The assertions, arguments, and conclusions are those of the author
and other contributors. They do not necessarily reflect the opinions
of the United States Holocaust Memorial Museum.

Library of Congress Cataloging-in-Publication data.

Aly, Götz, 1947–
  [Im Tunnel. English]
  The brief life of Marion Samuel, 1931–1943 / Götz Aly; translated by Ann Millin.
      p. cm.
  ISBN-13: 978-0-8050-7927-2
  ISBN-10: 0-8050-7927-0
  1. Samuel, Marion, 1931–1943.   2. Jewish children in the Holocaust—Germany.
I. Title.
  DS134.42.S26A6813   2007
  940.53'18092—dc22
  [B]   2007024463

First U.S. Edition 2007

Designed by Meryl Sussman Levavi
Printed in the United States of America
10 9 8 7 6 5 4 3 2 1

Contents

Preface

Ruth Kluger

THIS IS A WEIGHTY LITTLE BOOK, AS EASY TO READ AS it is difficult to forget. While the author is a prominent historian, his "heroine" is completely unknown—or was, until he set about rescuing her from obscurity. Marion Samuel, a German-Jewish child, was an ordinary victim of the Nazis' extermination policy, one of the faceless millions who were murdered as a matter of routine. Those who survived the Holocaust are always anything but ordinary or typical. They—or, since I am one of them, we—all owe our lives to some extraordinary circumstance, be it a twist of fate or a helping hand. Marion Samuel, by contrast, went to her inconspicuous death just as intended, according to the procedures laid down in monstrous yet bureaucratically unassuming files. Now Götz Aly has taken her forgotten name from a list, and, with no more than that name, he has pieced together the whole girl, her shape, her clothes, her face, her fears, her words, even finding old photographs that allow her to appear, literally, before our eyes.

In truth, it was not the author who chose Marion Samuel from a long list of deported Berlin Jews, but a foundation called Remembrance. Dedicated to researching the crimes of the Nazi era and commemorating its victims, the foundation awards an annual prize named after a randomly picked deportee, someone about whom nothing was known other than the bare shameful date of her deportation. When Götz Aly was awarded the Marion Samuel Prize, he responded with an act of empathy: putting his historian's skills to work, he retraced Marion's steps as closely as possible and followed every lead he could find, in an effort to rescue at least this one child from oblivion.

There is, of course, another girl who immediately comes to mind, another girl who died in a Nazi camp and whose life and death have been the subject of meticulous investigation. But Anne Frank was immortal even before the many books about her appeared, having left behind her world-famous diary. Marion Samuel, on the other hand, was a nobody, a blank page, someone who for a small number of years had a fragile claim to human existence.

I have to confess that I was especially moved by her story because I was born the same year as Marion, in 1931. Only three months older than me, she was gassed to death in Auschwitz-Birkenau in 1943, one year before I arrived there. By chance and luck I escaped the death machine and survived. As I read Marion's story, I couldn't help but ask: Why she and not I? And as I pondered this, I saw how the trite phrase "survivor's guilt" obscures the deeper and nobler feeling of survivor's sympathy.

Aly recounts his patient and painstaking search through the relevant archives, describes how he took out newspaper advertisements and looked for relatives in Germany and America, trying to find anyone who might have known this girl. He tells how he investigated the Samuel family's financial circumstances as well as their systematic impoverishment by the Nazi state, all perfectly legal. And as Aly unsentimentally tallies up the Samuels' dwindling resources, mere numbers take on an accusatory, almost satiric edge, for the accountants of the German Reich were particularly fastidious when it came to confiscated "Aryanized" property. With bitter irony he concludes that this particular deportation amounted to "a fiscal loss of 27.63 Reichsmarks." And he follows this up with a wry comment: "That was an exception."

But what is really at stake here is the unique life of one irreplaceable child. Against all probability, Götz Aly succeeded in resurrecting the image of Marion Samuel through the few old photos he found. These show a pretty little girl with big eyes. She's wearing a dress with a huge white collar and has an equally outsized bow in her hair. I look at the pictures and the child I once was perks up in my old woman's mind to say: "I'd never have worn a bow like that!" But mostly I think: Where was I when this or that was happening to her? Was her family like mine? Though Aly tells the story precisely and with restraint, he is free of the kind of pseudo-objectivity that precludes moral judgment. By simply presenting the facts with some occasional dry commentary, Aly reveals himself as the victim's advocate and the perpetrators' accuser.

The book's title restores a trace of Marion Samuel's voice. In a letter sent to the author, a former classmate recalls an exchange in 1938, in which the then seven-year-old Marion talked about her fears. She said: "People go into a tunnel in a mountain, and along the way there is a great hole and they all fall in and disappear." Marion's classmate adds: "I thought that she was acting a little crazy, and that this was a gruesome thing to say. . . . But she had probably overheard adults talking about things she could not fully comprehend, and then played out what she had heard in her child's fantasy." This rings true to me. At the time, the more adults tried to protect us, the more we children were desperate to understand why we and our families were being shunned and to know what awaited us in the future.

For Marion Samuel, the future was a brief life and a brutal end, followed by years of obscurity. In this little book, Götz Aly has accomplished a remarkable feat: he has vividly conjured up and restored to history the beginning of a life that was not to be. If only this work of commemoration could be done for all those who disappeared into the tunnel.

Foreword

Raul Hilberg,
recipient of the inaugural Marion Samuel prize

IN 1984, A CONFERENCE TOOK PLACE IN STUTTGART, GERMANY, to explore "The Murder of the Jews During the Second World War." At the dais, well-known researchers of that time presented their papers. In the first row experts offered comments. Then it was the turn of the anonymous audience, middle-aged men in the main. But in the rear a younger man posed a query, or perhaps he pointed to a problem. His was not an ordinary voice. He spoke with clarity, directness, and a confidence that contained the hint of a challenge. When we walked out, he approached me and handed me a small book that he had written with a coauthor. It dealt with a subject that no one, to my knowledge, had touched before: the attempt by the Nazi regime to track its entire population by means of Hollerith machines, an IBM technology. That young man was Götz Aly.

Nothing is scarcer in an academic discipline than a new idea.

From his initial study of demographers preoccupied with subjects such as "racial" Jews, half Jews, and quarter Jews, Aly went on to coauthor a larger book about planners, among them those men, rarely found in the indexes of works about Nazism, who thought about the exploitation, mass resettlements, and decimation of eastern European peoples. A pathbreaking work followed in which Aly placed ghettoization measures into a context of repatriations of ethnic Germans from the USSR and the search for a place for the "Final Solution" within the eastern European expanse.

Aly did not pursue the confining life of a professorial career. A master of the German language, he wrote short essays in a Berlin newspaper for a living, while joining another author in writing a book about the deportations of the Hungarian Jews and also producing a highly original work called *Hitler's Beneficiaries*. The German title of that book, *Hitlers Volksstaat*, conveys immediately that the beneficiaries were the German people. Soldiers and families with children were specially favored, and, to maintain the high volume of expenditures for the home front as well as the war, the state augmented its income by pillaging occupied territories and exhaustively expropriating the Jews.

The confiscation of property belonging to individual Jewish families is described in two of his subsequent publications. One is a coauthored case study in which several passages are devoted to the successive steps that were taken by German agencies in depriving a Jewish manufacturer of his assets, including a Berlin auction of a sofa, lamps, and porcelain. The other work is centered on Marion Samuel.

Aly's short account of the life and death of an eleven-year-old Jewish girl, with its family photos and facsimiles of German documents, exemplifies his consummate expertise. When the Marion

Samuel prize was created, no one knew anything about her save that she lived and died, but when Aly was selected to receive the award he resolved to begin what might easily have seemed to others a futile search for specifics. He found a variety of documents that chart Marion's life, among them an inventory of the modest belongings of the Samuel family. *Into the Tunnel* looks like a simple story, yet rarely are a perpetration and its impact so clearly shown between two covers. That he should even have thought of such a biography is remarkable.

Into the Tunnel

Chapter 1

Who Was This Marion Samuel?

IN 1951, THE GERMAN PHILOSOPHER RUDOLF SCHOTT-laender proposed that "the city of Berlin should designate a location where the Jewish children murdered under National Socialism" might be remembered. He noted, though, that such a memorial would be effective only "if it does not swim in the unbounded memory of all the victims of tyranny, the evil that is still happening and may yet happen, but rather is fixed on the zenith of inhumanity revealed in each and every murder of a million Jewish children."[1]

The proposal came to nothing in both halves of the then-divided Berlin. More than forty years later, Ingrid and Walther Seinsch took up the idea; they decided to commemorate the Jewish children who had been killed by establishing a historical research award. For the name of the prize, they picked a child at random

Name	Ort	Geburtsdatum	Status	Ziel
Samuel, Henriette, geb. Isaacsohn	Hamburg	28.07.62	verschollen	Minsk
Samuel, Herbert	Dortmund	11.05.10	07.01.43	Auschwitz
Samuel, Herbert	Rastatt	28.05.26	03.04.45	Mauthausen
Samuel, Hermann	Hamburg	27.01.81	29.07.42	Litzmannstadt/Lodz
Samuel, Hermann	Berlin	25.03.84	verschollen	Majdanek/Lublin
Samuel, Hermann	Rastatt	19.11.94	verschollen	Majdanek/Lublin
Samuel, Heron	Düsseldorf	29.06.78	verschollen	Minsk
Samuel, Hertha	Berlin	21.05.00	verschollen	Litzmannstadt/Lodz
Samuel, Hilde, geb. Lisser	Berlin	31.08.92	verschollen	Auschwitz
Samuel, Hildegard, geb. Wolff	Berlin	15.07.94	verschollen	Auschwitz
Samuel, Hugo	Berlin	07.07.79	verschollen	Riga
Samuel, Ida	Berlin	14.12.73	für tot erklärt	Theresienstadt
Samuel, Ida, geb. Tuteur	Winnweiler (1)	18.04.64	für tot erklärt	Auschwitz
Samuel, Ida, geb. Weil	Freudenburg	05.05.68	verschollen	Auschwitz
Samuel, Ilse	Bergzabern (1)	21.07.27	für tot erklärt	Auschwitz
Samuel, Ingeborg	Berlin	06.03.30	verschollen	Auschwitz
Samuel, Irma	Berlin	26.11.03	verschollen	Trawniki
Samuel, Isaak	Düsseldorf	29.07.70	verschollen	Minsk
Samuel, Isaak	Kassel	09.12.76	verschollen	Riga
Samuel, Isidor	Berlin	09.05.79	verschollen	Trawniki
Samuel, Jacob	Scharbach (1)	21.07.99	verschollen	Buchenwald
Samuel, Jakob	Berlin	21.06.98	verschollen	Auschwitz
Samuel, Jenny, geb. Josephsohn	Berlin	10.03.73	verschollen	Litzmannstadt/Lodz
Samuel, Jettka, geb. Haase	Berlin	14.06.71	verschollen	Auschwitz
Samuel, Johanna, geb. Berman	Erlenbach	02.03.95	verschollen	Gurs
Samuel, Johanna, geb. Levi-Deichmann	Hannover	28.12.74	verschollen	Riga
Samuel, Johanna, geb. Loewenthal	Berlin	14.11.88	verschollen	Auschwitz
Samuel, Josef	Berlin (2)	23.09.11	für tot erklärt	Mittelbau-Dora
Samuel, Josefine	Berlin	26.01.93	verschollen	Litzmannstadt/Lodz
Samuel, Joseph	Reichelsheim (1)	10.10.72	07.02.43	Theresienstadt
Samuel, Josephine	Linz am Rhein	11.12.70	22.08.42	Theresienstadt
Samuel, Juliane	Wunstorf	30.05.23	verschollen	Polen
Samuel, Julie, geb. Levy	Gersdorf (1)	14.03.80	verschollen	Auschwitz
Samuel, Julius	Erlenbach	03.11.27	verschollen	Gurs
Samuel, Julius	Köln	26.03.77	verschollen	Auschwitz
Samuel, Julius	Delmenhorst	09.03.78	für tot erklärt	Sobibor
Samuel, Julius	Bendorf	03.06.78	verschollen	Izbica
Samuel, Kaethe, geb. Petzal	Berlin	13.01.90	verschollen	Riga
Samuel, Karl	Thalfang	07.03.92	verschollen	Auschwitz
Samuel, Karola	Frechen	26.04.99	verschollen	Litzmannstadt/Lodz
Samuel, Karoline, geb. Levy	Hüls	18.03.77	verschollen	Minsk
Samuel, Klara, geb. Pappenheim	Berlin	19.12.73	verschollen	Riga
Samuel, Kurt	Ahlem	07.10.08	14.10.44	Theresienstadt
Samuel, Lazarus	Trier	18.04.61	30.08.42	Theresienstadt
Samuel, Leo	Bielefeld	23.04.12	verschollen	Theresienstadt
Samuel, Leon	Trittenheim (1)	09.04.09	verschollen	Auschwitz
Samuel, Leopold	Dortmund	13.07.72	27.12.43	Theresienstadt
Samuel, Lieselotte	Köln	25.08.23	verschollen	Auschwitz
Samuel, Lilli	Berlin	28.05.10	verschollen	Riga
Samuel, Lina	Fulda	13.03.87	verschollen	Polen
Samuel, Lotte	Philippsburg	31.07.12	verschollen	Auschwitz
Samuel, Louis	Fulda	22.03.01	für tot erklärt	Riga
Samuel, Louis	Berlin	20.11.68	28.11.42	Theresienstadt
Samuel, Louis	Münster	25.08.83	verschollen	Riga
Samuel, Margarete, geb. Aronheim	Berlin	06.07.77	verschollen	Riga
Samuel, Marianne, geb. Jakobs	Trittenheim	20.02.79	für tot erklärt	unbekannt
● Samuel, Marion	Berlin	27.07.31	verschollen	Auschwitz
Samuel, Martha, geb. Pincus	München	20.10.62	verschollen	Riga
Samuel, Martin	Bremen	18.04.31	28.07.42	Minsk
Samuel, Martin	Bremen	06.08.73	07.01.43	Theresienstadt
Samuel, Martin	Berlin	18.08.86	verschollen	Auschwitz
Samuel, Martin	Berlin	08.03.99	verschollen	Auschwitz
Samuel, Mathilde, geb. Meyer	Köln	13.04.85	verschollen	Auschwitz
Samuel, Mathilde, geb. Solms	Berlin	09.07.75	verschollen	Riga
Samuel, Max	Hamburg	11.04.24	verschollen	Riga
Samuel, Max	Erlenbach	10.01.85	verschollen	Gurs
Samuel, Max	Hannover	12.04.97	verschollen	Riga
Samuel, Maximilian	Frechen	15.09.80	verschollen	Auschwitz
Samuel, Meinhard	Hüls	02.08.82	verschollen	Riga
Samuel, Melanie, geb. Levy	Trier	22.07.97	verschollen	Auschwitz
Samuel, Meyer	Linz am Rhein	05.12.68	verschollen	Minsk
Samuel, Mirtyl	Trier	08.04.58	verschollen	Minsk
Samuel, Moses	Trittenheim (1)	19.07.77	für tot erklärt	unbekannt
Samuel, Paul	Trittenheim (1)	10.12.10	verschollen	Majdanek/Lublin

from a memorial book for deported German Jews: Marion Samuel. All that was known about her was the place and year of her birth—Arnswalde, 1931—and the date of her deportation from Berlin to Auschwitz: March 3, 1943.[2] A detailed history published by the city provides only a slightly more extensive entry: "Samuel, Marion, b. July 27, 1931, in Arnswalde, Brandenburg; [Berlin-]Prenzlauer Berg, Rhinower Street 11; transported March 3, 1943, Auschwitz; place of death: Auschwitz; presumed dead."[3]

At the end of November 2002, I received a brief message from Walther Seinsch: "We would like to honor you with next year's Marion Samuel Prize." I thought, who was this Marion Samuel? I had heard the name somewhere before, and at first I vaguely supposed she might have been some Jewish intellectual of great promise who was murdered while still young. Eventually, I found an article on the Internet that I myself—strange as it may sound—had written in 1999, when Raul Hilberg received the inaugural Marion Samuel Prize. In the article I speculated that, most probably, on account of her age Marion Samuel was "poisoned with Zyklon B" in Auschwitz "immediately after her arrival." Furthermore, I said, it was likely that "her father had performed forced labor in a Berlin factory as a so-called armaments Jew. These Jews were replaced by young Poles who were brought to Berlin."[4] As I know today, both of these speculations were correct.

OPPOSITE: The listing for Marion Samuel on page 1289 of the German national archive's memorial book of the murdered German Jews. "Verschollen," literally *lost* or *missing*, denotes those whose exact fate is not known. "Für tot erklärt" means *declared dead*. The memorial book is not comprehensive; there are no entries, for instance, for Marion Samuel's uncle Werner or her grandmother Jenny, who were both murdered after being deported from Königsberg in 1942.

Lfde. Nr.	Vorname	Familienname bei Frauen auch Mädchenname	Geburtstag, Geburtsmonat, Geburtsjahr	Geburtsort und -kreis (siehe Erläuterung III)	War oder ist einer der vier Großelternteile der Rasse nach Volljude? (Ja oder nein) (siehe Erläuterung IV)				Haben Si... Hochschul... Fachschul... abgeschlo... (Ja oder...
					Großvater	Großmutter	Großvater	Großmutter	
					väterlicherseits		mütterlicherseits		
	1	2		3	4	6	6	7	8	9

A. Sämtliche Anwesende

	Paul	Schmitz	8.10.1885	Marklissa, Krs. Lauban	nein	nein	nein	nein	nein
2.	Marta	Schmitz, geb Zwralka	18.9.1888	Hennigsfeld, Krs. Stolen	nein	nein	nein	nein	nein
3.	Hermann	Schmitz	11.2.1829	Magdeburg	nein	nein	nein	nein	nein
4.	Anna	Kawozek	2.10.1865	Wogher, Krs. Stolen	nein	nein	nein	nein	nein
5.	Alfred	Jung	16.1.1889	Schönebeck, Krs. Calw a.S.	nein	nein	nein	nein	ja
6.	Franz	Müller	20.5.1912	Danzig	nein	nein	nein	nein	ja
1.	Sally	Cohn	8.8.1886	Lodz, Poln	ja	ja	ja	ja	nein
2.	Henriette	Cohn, geb. Oppenheimer	20.3.1884	Breslau	ja	nein	ja	nein	nein
3.	Georg	Cohn	26.10.1905	Breslau	ja	ja	nein	nein	ja
4.	Ruth	Schmidt, geb. Cohn	20.9.1907	Berlin	ja	ja	nein	nein	nein
5.	Elsbeth	Schmidt	25.1.1909	Berlin	nein	nein	nein	nein	nein
6.	Martha	Nicholim	24.5.1880	Kaufheun, Krs. Göldberg	nein	nein	nein	nein	nein
1.	Egon Israel	Samuel	6.11.1908	Hergberg...	ja	ja	ja	ja	nein
2.	Hetty Sara	Samuel geb Neumel	28.12.1908	Aussald...	ja	ja	ja	ja	nein
3.	Marion Sara	Samuel	27.7.1931	" Ls. Aussald	ja	ja	ja	ja	nein
4.									
5.									
6.									
7.									
8.									
9.									
10.									

B. Vorübergehend abwesende Mitglieder der Haushaltung

Beispiel	Richard	Schmitt	19.11.1904	Hanau	nein	nein	nein	nein	nein
1.									
2.									
3.									
4.									

Bescheinigung: Daß die Angaben vollständig und nach bestem Wissen gemacht worden sind, bescheinigt:

Wohnung:

Hier bitte Ihre Unterschrift:

(Unterschrift des Haushaltungsvorstandes, seines Vertreters ...)

On that same evening in November 2002, I decided that I wanted to find out more. The award ceremony was scheduled for May 2003, and I resolved that my acceptance speech should be a biographical sketch of the short life of Marion Samuel. I immediately came up against difficulties. Marion's whole family had been murdered in Auschwitz. They were ordinary, and therefore left behind few traces. The entry for Marion Samuel in the Berlin databank of material assembled for the memorial book of the deported Jews produced some information about her parents, where the

Supplementary survey form from the May 1939 census, on which Ernst Samuel was required—under threat of punishment—to note whether the four grandparents of each member of the family were Jewish "according to race." The fourfold *yes* answers meant that, according to the 1935 Nuremberg Laws, Ernst, Cilly, and Marion were "full Jews." The form is signed "Ernst Israel Samuel." *(Bundesarchiv, Berlin)*

family had lived in Berlin, and which schools Marion had attended. Still, it seemed almost impossible to gather enough evidence to provide a more detailed picture.

I turned to old Berlin address and telephone books, and to archived bureaucratic records. The German federal archive holds a collection of the special file cards that were created for each Jewish student. Marion's card, for example, notes that she was inoculated against smallpox on June 4, 1932, and allowed me to reconstruct her progress in school with some accuracy.[5] At the archive I also found the Samuel family's responses to the May 17, 1939, census. Families were required to answer the question, "Was or is one of the respondent's four grandparents a full Jew?" Instructions for filling out this section of the questionnaire read, "Racial status alone, not confessional affiliation, is definitive." On the basis of the answers—supposedly confidential—local authorities created special registration systems that later enabled police to track down the victims and made identifications error-free, unlike those based on denunciations or "racial assessments." For the historian, this largely intact file—with its birthplaces and birth dates, its names and addresses of family members—renders visible people who were soon to disappear almost without a trace.[6]

German Jews assembled for deportation were required by the Nazi government, acting out of a mixture of greed and bureaucratic thoroughness, to fill out a property declaration. The Berlin expropriation files have been preserved, and in the case of the Samuel family there are three sets of forms. The records note that their rental apartment had been sealed. They track the recovery of even the smallest of debts and include an assessment of the apartment's inventory, carried out by an executor of the upper court. The documentation concludes with a balance statement. Whatever funds remained were transferred to the German Reich: that is, they were nationalized for the benefit of the German majority.[7]

Beyond these specific administrative records, we can also get important clues to the conditions that shaped Marion Samuel's life from the detailed historical monographs that have been produced in an impressive variety over the past two decades. These accounts—about the Factory Action to which the Samuel family fell victim, for example, or about the Jewish schools in Berlin—have allowed me to include memories of contemporaries who crossed Marion's path, or who lived near her or her parents or underwent similar experiences. In addition, most of the important historical dates for the Jews who once lived in Marion's hometown of Arnswalde can be found in the *Heimatgruss-Rundbrief aus den ehemaligen Kirchengemeinden im Kreis Arnswalde (Neumark)*, a voluminous, lovingly created journal of the Germans who were expelled when that town became part of Poland after the war. The journal appears four times a year, and is entering its seventh decade of publication. Fifteen years ago, its editors decided to include the previously unmentioned fate of the Jews of Arnswalde. The Jews were, after all, the first to be expelled from the city, hunted by those who would themselves become refugees in February 1945.

After I was unable to find further information in the archives, I published an article in the local section of the *Berliner Zeitung* in February 2003, titled "Who Knew Marion Samuel?"[8] The single response came from Hilma Krüger (b. Kaul), who had gone to elementary school with Marion in 1937. She mentioned that a class photograph was taken at the beginning of the semester, but that her own copy had been destroyed in the bombings. Hilma Krüger was able to recall the names of many of Marion Samuel's former classmates, but none of the names of these girls were to be found in the Berlin telephone book. I therefore published a second appeal, titled "Class Photograph Sought." After a brief introduction about the class taught by Frau Mollmann at the public school in the Sonnenburger Strasse in 1937, the article continued: "Because all the students in that class were girls who later married, their maiden names do not appear in the telephone book. We are thus dependent upon the help of our attentive readers to find these women. Among the girls, all born in 1930/31, who belonged to the class were Marianne Hübner, Ingrid Klaf(f)t, Inge Knapp, Gisela Lampel, Inge

Lexow, Gisela Schäfer, Helga Korzenburg, Vera Wetzel, Traute Zinke, Tamara May, Brigitte Fischer, Gisela Jonitz, Helga Kassube(a), Inge Klammt, Annelise Klawe, Inge Kretsch, Regina Luc(z)inski, Ruth Mattern, Anneliese Wischer, and Gisela Schulz.

"The list is not complete and may contain some errors, but Frau Hilma K., born Kaul, has a clear memory which is supported by the list of confirmands of the Gethsemane Church. The confirmation of girls born in that year took place on March 18, 1945, during a Volkssturm swearing-in ceremony and shortly before a heavy bombardment of the area. I would be grateful for correspondence with anyone who can provide clues."[9]

The very next day the twin brother of one of the former students contacted me—and he had a copy of the class photograph. Hilma Krüger immediately recognized Marion Samuel. The unknown victim had a face once more.

Marion Samuel died in Auschwitz on March 4, 1943. Her parents also perished there. The majority of her other close relatives likewise fell victim to destruction. I wanted to find the few who had survived, but this was not a simple task. I knew neither their first names nor their dates of birth, and Samuel is a very common last name. This situation was complicated by the fact that both the maiden and married names of Marion's mother were Samuel. In addition, a great part of the story had played out in Arnswalde, which today is in Poland, and in the formerly East Prussian Königsberg, now the Russian city of Kaliningrad. The residential registrations and municipal marriage records had been destroyed by fire at the end of the war. Despite all my efforts, by the time that I received the Marion Samuel prize in May 2003 I still knew almost nothing about Marion Samuel's extended family.

The class photograph from the 117th Elementary School in Berlin, taken around Easter in 1937. Marion Samuel, with the black ribbon in her hair, stands directly in the middle of the photograph. Hilma Krüger (b. Kaul) is at the far left of the second row from the front, her head tilted to the side. Gertrud Förster (b. Novak), whose twin brother provided the photo, is the girl with braids at the right side of the same row.

Restitution forms at the Berlin reparations bureau, however, had hinted that the Samuels might have been related to someone named Pohl in the town of Greifswald. I wrote to the Greifswald registry office to find out if they had any further information. A week after the award ceremony, the registry put me in touch with Erika Dünkel, who lived near Berlin. "Yes," she said when I telephoned her, "Marion Samuel was my cousin." I sent her a copy of the speech I had delivered at the award ceremony, which had been published in the *Berliner Zeitung*.[10] She was quite moved, and confirmed the details: "The story has been written just as my mother

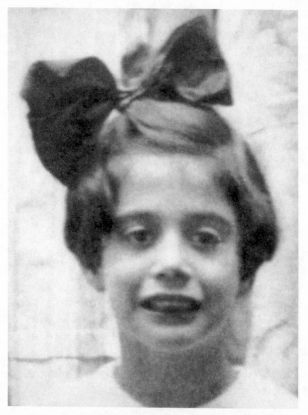

Marion Samuel (enlargement from the class photo)

told it to us." Erika Dünkel's mother—Helene Pohl, born Samuel, an aunt of Marion Samuel's on her mother's side—had survived the war with her children in what was known as a "privileged mixed marriage" in Königsberg, where they later came under Soviet rule. They had been saved only because Helene Pohl's Christian husband repeatedly rebuffed government pressure to divorce her, for which he was eventually incarcerated in a labor camp. The Pohl family was not reunited until 1947.

From the property declaration submitted by Marion Samuel's

mother, I knew that one of her brothers had emigrated to the United States. I had been unable to discover his name, but Erika Dünkel pointed me to one of several names I had drawn from the reparations file: Arthur Samuel. Men by this name were and are numerous in the United States, and I spent two months checking these leads. As it turned out, only a few of them came from Germany, and I eventually learned that the Arthur Samuel I had been looking for had died in New York in 1985. Of what use is an address in the United States when the person who lived there died twenty years earlier?

Erika Dünkel knew that Arthur had a son, Manfred, who was born in Germany and appears with other relatives in an old family photograph. However, contact with Manfred had broken off after the death of his mother thirty-five years before. "Manfred" could have become "Fred" or "Freddy," and Erika thought that Freddy had probably served in the army and might possibly have a son by the name of David. She did not have any more information than that, though, and even a search performed with the help of the specialists of the Survivors Registry at the United States Holocaust Memorial Museum in Washington produced nothing.

After many detours, assorted hypotheses that turned out to be false, and lots of telephone conversations with various people named Samuel ("No, we are Christians!"), I finally found Fred Samuel via the Internet. The telephone books from each of the American states contained hundreds of Samuels named Fred and David; searching through all of them would have been futile. But somewhere in the depths of switchboard.com I stumbled upon listings in which a person's age as well as name is given. There I identified four seventy-year-old Fred Samuels, one of whom was Fred M. Samuel. The "M." could be, I surmised, a sentimental reminder of "Manfred."

He was indeed the person I had been looking for, although the middle initial turned out to be just a lucky coincidence. The family lived in a large Jewish community twenty miles from New York City. A week later, Fred Moritz Samuel, his wife, Carole, and their son, David, picked me up at the train station in Newark, New Jersey. We spent two days together, at the end of which we were joined by a reporter from the local press.[11] Fred Samuel knew little about the relatives on his father's side of the family, only that they had been murdered during the Holocaust. He showed me the family photograph that his cousin Erika had described, but he could not tell me anything about it. In the photograph, Marion looks much more relaxed than in the school picture, but she is wearing the same dress with a collar and a similar ribbon in her hair. Her parents stand behind her, in the center of the family group. Fred is in the front row next to Marion; on her other side is Erika Dünkel's brother Wolfgang, who died in an accident in 1996. A detail from that photograph is on the cover of this book, and the photo itself is on pages 86–87.

In a way, the fact that I found both of Marion's living relatives rather late in my search proved to be an advantage. Had Fred and Erika been able to speak with me right at the beginning of my research, I would have been spared many detours—but I also might not have been driven to publish the newspaper articles seeking Marion's classmates and the school photograph, and I might not have checked a hard-to-find refugee newspaper for information on the Jewish families of Arnswalde. Thanks to all the twists and turns of my search, the sketchy history of Marion Samuel became clearer.

I could find no living relatives from the paternal side of Marion Samuel's family. Marion's father had five siblings; two of them (his brother Kurt and his sister Margarethe) were murdered during the Holocaust, and his three other siblings all died childless. However, my conversations with Fred Samuel and Erika Dünkel made it possible for me to describe the very different fates of the members of this Jewish family under persecution. Their history, which includes brief accounts of everyone pictured alongside Erika, Fred, and Marion in that family photo, is told in the last part of this book. Loyal, modest Germans, who for generations worked, paid taxes, and celebrated their holidays, they were suddenly forced to flee from the comfort of a small town in eastern Germany into the anonymity of larger cities—to Königsberg, Berlin, New York. Although emigration allowed some 70 percent of German Jews to escape the Holocaust, many in the Samuel family were not so fortunate.

During the past twenty years, Fred and Carole Samuel have traveled widely. They have been in Europe many times, and they visited Auschwitz without knowing which members of Fred's family died there. They never, however, entered Germany. On the second day of my stay with the Samuels, we decided to telephone Erika Dünkel in Berlin. Fred Samuel no longer speaks German: as a consequence of the trauma he experienced at the age of six, he lost every memory of his childhood in Arnswalde and Königsberg. Not even a memory of his voyage to the United States remains. Erika Dünkel does not know English. I encouraged them to try simply speaking with each other in their respective languages. On the telephone—very slowly, almost without an accent—Fred Samuel, speaking to his cousin, once again found a few German words.

Chapter 2

Once Upon a Time in Arnswalde
and Ueckermünde

MARION SAMUEL WAS BORN ON JULY 27, 1931, THE ONLY child of Ernst and Cilly Samuel. The family lived in the town of Arnswalde in the Neumark region, in the eastern part of Brandenburg, about a hundred miles northeast of Berlin. (Today the town is located in Poland and is known as Choszczno.) Marion's parents, who by coincidence already shared the same last name, were married in 1929 and lived with Cilly Samuel's extended family.[12]

Cilly Samuel herself was born in Arnswalde in 1908. She had one sister and three brothers, of whom two—Martin and Werner—died in the Holocaust, as did her mother, Jenny Samuel, born Marcuse. Cilly's father, Carl Samuel, died before the deportations began.[13] The third brother, the aforementioned Arthur, was able to emigrate to the United States with his wife and son in time to

The five children of Carl and Jenny Samuel. Clockwise from bottom left: Helene, circa 1915; Werner, Arthur, and Cilly, circa 1930; Martin, in 1937.

escape deportation. The sister, Helene, was married to a Christian and survived the war in Germany with her children.

Carl and Jenny Samuel, Marion's grandparents, ran a department store in Arnswalde: "W. A. Samuel. Manufacturing, Ready-to-Wear, Shoes." The business was housed in a building at Am Markt 9 owned by the family, and could be reached by telephone at number 245.[14] The firm had been founded by Marion's great-grandfather, Wolf Abraham Samuel, in the town of Werben (near Pyritz) in the Pomerania region, where he had settled. Carl and Jenny Samuel moved to Arnswalde with the business shortly after Helene's birth in 1896, and their son Arthur took over the company in 1932. It seems very likely that Ernst Samuel, Cilly's husband, also worked in the store.[15]

Marion Samuel's birthplace in Arnswalde, at Am Markt 9. The "Berliner Warenhaus" (Berlin Department Store) inscription on the family's shop is at the center of the photo. (*Der Kreis Arnswalde in alten Ansichten, Wunstorf, 1997*)

We can get some sense of the Samuel family's life in the early decades of the twentieth century from the investigations of Wolfgang Palm, a dedicated amateur chronicler of Arnswalde who has written numerous articles for the *Heimatgruss-Rundbrief* journal. In 2000, for instance, Palm spoke with Fritz Jahn, a pensioner who remembered Cilly Samuel from her days at the private academy for girls run by Fräulein Pohl in the Wilhelmsplatz. (This academy later became the town's public middle school for girls.) According to Jahn's account, anti-Semitism was not an issue during Cilly's school years. The Jewish students in Arnswalde, he said, "were not treated any differently than the other girls."[16]

One might wonder whether this recollection, from an elderly man looking back at his childhood days, casts too kind a light upon the past. However, his memory is supported by a recent letter from a Jewish native of Arnswalde named Ruth Bartal. Bartal, the daughter of horse trader Isidor Duschnitzki, was born in 1922 and attended the same school as Cilly Samuel. As she wrote in 1993 from her present-day residence in Israel, "I have only happy memories of my school days. For ten years, I was the sole Jewish child in the class, but I never heard a single mean remark. Our headmistress, Frieda Vonberg, the teachers, and my schoolmates were all friendly and good to us." She added, "Today I think of Arnswalde with nostalgia. My parents and grandparents lie buried there, although the cemetery itself has been destroyed. Every year, I long to return once again to Arnswalde. There is no denying that my roots are there. I mourn for our lovely, peaceful city and for its many, many decent citizens. I would like to send my schoolmates heartfelt greetings and wish them all health and peace."[17]

Until 1933, the Jews of Arnswalde indeed lived as respected citizens of the city. They worked as confectioners and cigar makers,

Nur zu Militärzwecken brauchbar.

Daß in dem Geburtsregister des hiesigen ... unterzeichneten Amtsgerichts ... Pränn 64 folgender Vermerk eingetragen steht:

Laut Verfügung vom 2 December 1868, ... IV fol. 184 ... betreffend die Geburten des hiesigen, ist die Ehefrau des Kaufmann Wolf Abraham **Samuel** Henriette geborene Wilczek zu Werben, ... ember 1868 ...
November Ein tausend achthundert sechzig von einem Kinde männlichen Geschlechts entbunden, welches den Vornamen „**Carl**" erhalten hat. Eingetragen zu Stargard, den zweiten December Ein tausend achthundert sechzig ...

... December ...

wird hiermit amtlich bescheinigt.

Stargard i/Pom, den 11 Januar 1858

Königl. Amtsgericht, Abth. ...

...

Attest.

Ext. III 8
A. G. – II. 165
Formular No. 11. Adlerbogen zu Attesten.

R.

The Höhere Töchterschule (High School for Girls) in Arnswalde, circa 1910. Helene Samuel, wearing a necklace, is second from left in the third row from the top.

OPPOSITE: Carl Samuel was born before the establishment of state registration bureaus. His birth was recorded instead by the local Jewish community, and confirmed by the local district court in this 1880 certificate. The note above the eagle, possibly added later when Carl had received his draft notice, says, "Unsuitable for military service." The document reads:

> Certificate. The birth register of the Jews of the undersigned district court records the following, Book I, page 64: According to the hearing of 2 December 1868, volume IV page 184 of the section concerning Jewish births, the wife of the businessman Wolf Abraham Samuel, Henriette, born Wilizek, was delivered of a male child on 17 November 1868—the seventeenth of November eighteen hundred sixty-eight—who received the first name "Carl." Registered by Stargard on the second of December, eighteen hundred sixty-eight.
> [Signed:] Rhuler.
> [Signed:] Streuber, Recorder.
> Hereby officially certified. Stargard, Pom[erania], the 11th of January 1880.
> Royal District Court, Section V.

furriers and butchers, dealers in grain, hides, leather, raw wool, and horses; they ran ironware stores and candy shops, depots for agricultural supplies and guesthouses for travelers. We find their names in the town records: Abraham Abraham, Emma Mannheim, Wilhelm Arenholz, Amadeus Menasse, Benno Schöps, Martha Gottfeld, Salli Jachmann, Frau Moses and Frau Silberstein, Ludwig Itzig and the widow of Julius Reich. In 1912, grain merchant and banker Eduard Abrahamowsky provided 40 percent of the funds for the Schnitterinnen fountain in the middle of the marketplace that, together with the Gothic-style brick church, became the symbol of the city.[18]

When change came, it came rapidly. Alfred Jachmann, an Arnswalde native whose entire family was eventually deported to Auschwitz, recalled that by 1935 "a fierce, uncontrolled anti-Semitism had spread across the entire province."[19] Meanwhile, according to Emilie Holz, who like Fritz Jahn was interviewed by Wolfgang Palm for the *Heimatgruss-Rundbrief*, the dry goods business owned by the Samuels was "suddenly closed soon after 1933."[20] The *Heimatgruss-Rundbrief* does not have any more information about this closure, but further details can be found in a handwritten draft account of his experiences that Arthur Samuel prepared after arriving in New York. "I took over the business after my marriage in 1932," he wrote, "but was forced by the boycott and by Nazi persecution to give it up in 1934." The last half of this sentence, through which a line has been drawn, replaces a more exact variant in which he wrote that he ran the business "only for a short time" because "after Hitler's rise to power," in Arnswalde just as in the rest of Germany, "all Jewish businesses were boycotted." Then, "for the second time, right after the New Year in 1934, all businesses and all storefront windows, as well as other windows, were demolished." After that, Arthur concluded, "I was forced to close the firm."

The wave of animosity swept up all the Jews in Arnswalde, regardless of their social standing. One of the smashed store windows, for example, was the newly installed display window of Julius Joelsohn—a neighbor of the Samuels who was a well-respected shopkeeper, "5' 9" tall, strong, a stutterer, a good man who had served in Field Artillery Regiment 18 in Frankfurt am Oder."[21] Another telling case is documented in the minutes of a discussion conducted in August 1935 in the office of Hjalmar Schacht, the president of the national Reichsbank. According to this record, the director of the branch bank in Arnswalde had been seen shopping in the store of a Jew who had been a corporal in the war and had received the Iron Cross. Consequently, local Nazi party activists published a photograph of the director in the Nazi weekly *Der Stürmer,* captioned, "He who does business with Jews is a traitor to the people!" The newspaper was displayed in triple-windowed display cases all around the town. Schacht immediately registered a protest, labeling the incident an act of the "highest perfidiousness and nastiness." The representative of the propaganda ministry replied that he saw "nothing reprehensible" in the action taken by the local party activists. The Interior Minister, meanwhile, conceded that such "unauthorized isolated incidents" were a problem, and declared that his ministry would soon issue a series of specific directives concerning the "Jewish question" that would "resolve it on a fully legal basis."[22] And indeed the ministry did so, with the Nuremberg Laws that were announced the following month.

After the firm was closed, Carl and Arthur Samuel sold the

company's building to the municipal savings bank, which stood next door. The bank had the building torn down in 1935, but its foundations remained intact for more than a decade, through the entire war. Part of the reason for the delay in rebuilding was a continuing debate among the city councillors about the route of a new street that would better connect the Mühlentorstrasse and the former Judenstrasse ("Jews' Road")—now renamed for Georg Buchholzer, an early champion of the local Reformation.[23] This idea of running a road through the space where the Samuel family's building had been is in accord with a later decree of Hitler's, whereby the "possessions and property" of Jews were to be transferred directly into community property.

The regulations for implementing this decree made it clear that as much as possible, Jewish plots of land were to be used to "widen roads or to lay out new streets"; the land owned by Jews could also be utilized for "plazas, green spaces, and sports venues." In other instances, suitable buildings were to be used for such purposes as "offices, schools, Hitler Youth hostels, children's homes, homes for the elderly, Red Cross installations." Later on, during the war, undeveloped land seized from Jews was also used for "the construction of shelters for those who had lost their homes to the bombings."[24]

In 1938, all Jewish students were required to leave the public schools. As a resident of Arnswalde recounted after the war: "One morning our teacher, Fräulein Haasch, entered the classroom with the words, 'Gerda Jachmann will not be coming to school any longer.' No one asked why. I told my parents and they said, 'Don't brood on it, the Jews are all going to America.' Only later did I realize that my parents had not told me the truth."[25] Gerda Jachmann—the sister of Alfred Jachmann, and the best student in the class—died in Auschwitz after being deported there in March 1943.

Leo Duschnitzki, the brother of Cilly Samuel's classmate Ruth Duschnitzki (later Bartal) and a childhood friend of Cilly's brother Werner, remembers the situation getting increasingly worse. "We were threatened more and more; some of our possessions were confiscated, and the other children were forbidden to visit us." Despite the upstanding reputation of his family, the windows of their home were broken—although, Leo points out, "Afterward our house was full of friends wishing to console us."[26] In the end, Leo and Ruth Duschnitzki left Arnswalde only because their father was killed in a railroad accident near Berlinchen. "As strange as it sounds, that accident saved our lives," says Ruth Bartal today. "My father would never have left Arnswalde, if only on account of his friends and classmates. After all, my mother's seven brothers all earned the Iron Cross in the First World War."[27]

On November 9, 1938, the synagogue in Arnswalde, known to all as "the Temple," went up in flames. The Jewish men of the city were arrested and held for some months in the Sachsenhausen concentration camp. "When my father returned after nine months there," remembers Alfred Jachmann, "he was no longer himself. Our family was obliged to leave the city and settle in extremely cramped lodgings in Berlin."[28] How the destruction of Arnswalde's Jews played out—who took part, which fire brigade held back, who profited directly from the actual persecution—is not detailed in the *Heimatgruss-Rundbrief*. The journal did, however, unearth a notice from the November 11, 1938, edition of the *Ostland-Zeitung* newspaper: "Change of ownership: the property of the Jewish produce dealer Falk in the Hohentorstrasse has been deeded to Hermann Lenz, businessman. The transfer of ownership is effective immediately."[29]

The considerable success of the state-mandated hatred can be measured by statistics. In 1925, ninety-seven Jews resided in the city. By May 1939, when the population of Arnswalde was approximately fourteen thousand, only twelve remained.[30]

The Jewish congregation in Arnswalde had belonged to the very oldest in Brandenburg. Its cemetery ("Judenkiever") was the second-oldest in the whole region, with its existence documented since the early fourteenth century. The decree of the city council of Arnswalde from September 7, 1321, concerning the rights and duties of the Jews, belongs to the earliest examples in Germany of this type of record. When measured against the conditions for Jews of that time, it is also strikingly liberal. "The synagogue and the buildings belonging to the community," read the councillors' conclusion, "shall be the free property of the Jews in perpetuity, and they shall pay no tax, and shall remain free from rendering any services—with the exception of the night watch, which they will perform together with us. . . . For this they shall pay us yearly two marks of silver; one mark on St. Martin's Day, the other on St. Walburga's Day. . . . No one shall any longer hinder the Jews in the slightest from entering or leaving our city."[31]

This admirable decree also extended to the perpetual protection of the Jewish cemetery against vandalism. From then on, for more than six hundred years, the Jewish dead rested under the spruces and leafy trees in the cemetery's somewhat removed and sheltered ground. (This place of peace, which represented a long if not always harmonious period in German Jewish-Christian relations, was preserved in watercolors by Hans Salewsky, who taught drawing at the Arnswalde high school from 1930 to 1938.) During the 1943–44 school year, however, with the participation of several classes, the cemetery's surrounding wall and the funeral hall were

Heimatgruß-Rundbrief

Aus den ehemaligen Kirchengemeinden im Kreis Arnswalde (Neumark)

53. Jahrgang   Juli / August / September 2000   250. Folge

Judenfriedhof in Arnswalde
Gemälde von Hans Salewsky (1901–1940), der von 1930 bis 1938 Zeichenlehrer an der Arnswalder Oberschule
war. Es handelt sich um die einzige, erhaltene Ansicht dieses ältesten Judenfriedhofs der Mark Brandenburg
(erste Erwähnung 1320).
Dieses Bild sollte schon in Folge 249 erscheinen, war leider nicht verfügbar.

Hans Salewsky's watercolor of the Jewish cemetery in Arnswalde torn down and the stones used to build a shelter for people who had become homeless in the bombings. The final destruction of both the Jewish and the Christian cemeteries was completed after 1945 under Polish rule.[32]

Alfred Jachmann visited his native city in the late 1980s. He remembers: "I said to my wife and son, 'Come, I will show you the Jewish cemetery on the Stadtberg.' I found the location, but the cemetery was no more. Nor was there a sign saying that it had once been there. Nature has reclaimed the cemetery. It was completely destroyed; today there are only broken stones. That is all you can see." Everything was overgrown with ivy and underbrush, he said. "Nothing in the city recalled that Jews had once lived there."[33]

Marion Samuel's father, Ernst, came from the town of Ueckermünde in the Vorpommern (West Pomerania) region. He was born there in 1905, the son of Adolf Samuel, a businessman, and his wife, Helene (née Levy). His parents kept a small shop in the main thoroughfare of the business district, which closely resembled the one in Arnswalde owned by Cilly Samuel's family and which had the "largest turnover" in Ueckermünde before World War I. The shop was located in a modest two-story building with guttered windows that was owned by Ernst Samuel's family. "Manufactured Goods and Clothing, Warehouse, Shoes—Adolf Samuel" was painted in great black letters on the white background of the gable end. Ernst Samuel eventually joined his father in the business, but it was sold in 1931 to one Gustav Laue, who kept a grocery store there until the 1950s. (The "Adolf Samuel" inscription could still be read well after the war.) Later, the building was converted into a consumer sales office for household and electronic wares. Today it is a shoe store.[34]

Adolf Samuel's shop in Ueckermünde *(Heinz Grosskopf, Ueckermünde)*

Ernst Samuel, in 1937

Ernst Samuel's birth certificate has a notation in the margin: "Ueckermünde, December 30, 1938. In accordance with section 2 of the Second Regulation for the Implementation of the Law Regarding the Changing of Family Names and Given Names of August 17, 1938, the hereby designated Ernst Samuel has taken the middle name 'Israel.' Declared on December 9, 1938, at the Registry Office; effective from January 1, 1939. (Signed) Kohtz." The middle name "Israel" was imposed upon all Jewish men; for Jewish women, "Sara" was added. This occurred parallel to the introduction of the Jewish identity card, which contained a passport photo and the fingerprints of both index fingers. Both the identity card and the additional name served to further the systematic registration, social isolation, and control of the Jewish minority in Germany.

Beneath that official notice in the margin of Ernst Samuel's birth certificate, there is a second remark: "Ueckermünde, Febru-

OPPOSITE: Ernst Samuel's birth certificate. The certificate itself, in the left-hand column, reads:

No. 192

Ueckermünde, 9 November 1905

Before the undersigned registry official, the person known as the merchant Adolf Samuel, who lives in Ueckermünde at Ueckerstrasse 19, of the Mosaic religion, appeared and declared that to his wife Helene Samuel, b. Levy, of the Mosaic religion, who lives with him in Ueckermünde, a boy was born on the sixth of November of the year one thousand nine hundred and five, at about a quarter to six in the morning, and that the child received the first name of Ernst. Read and confirmed,

Adolf Samuel

Registry Official
(signature)

The handwritten remarks in the right-hand margin and the stamp at the bottom of the certificate are described in the text above and on page 79. *(Standesamt Ueckermünde)*

A.

Nr. *192*

Uerkermünde am *9ᵗᵉ November* 1905

Vor dem unterzeichneten Standesbeamten erschien heute, der Persönlichkeit

nach _____

_____ bekannt,

der *Kaufmann Adolf Samuel*

wohnhaft in *Uerkermünde, ___ Straße 14*

_____ mosaischer _____ Religion, und zeigte an, daß von der

Selma Samuel geborne Levy, seiner

Ehefrau _____

_____ mosaischer Religion,

wohnhaft *bei ihm dem Anzeigenden*

zu *Uerkermünde in der gemeinsamen Wohnung*

am _____ *fünf* ᵗᵉⁿ *November* des Jahres

tausend neunhundert *und fünf* _____ vormittags

um *fünf drei viertel* Uhr ein *Knabe*

geboren worden sei und daß das Kind *den* Vornamen

Ernst

erhalten habe. _____

_____

Vorgelesen, genehmigt und *unterschrieben* _____

_____ *Adolf Samuel* _____

Der Standesbeamte.

Fritz

Versterben: am 04.05.1943
Standesamt *Sonderstandesamt Arolsen,*
Abt. Auschwitz Nr. *507/1963*

ary 12, 1951. The note of December 30, 1938, is to be treated as though never written. The decree of August 1938 is declared immoral. (By decree of the President of Mecklenburg-Vorpommern, September 1, 1945.) Gabriel, Registrar."[35]

While the Jewish community in Arnswalde can be traced back to the fourteenth century, there were no Jews at all in Ueckermünde until the 1812 Prussian emancipation edict, which—in theory, at least—made Prussian Jews into full citizens and did away with most of the restrictive racial laws against them. Although the emancipation edict was partially repealed in 1814, the economic enticements of Prussia, combined with a fear of pogroms in the east, drew a trickle of Jewish families from Russia and Poland over the course of the nineteenth century. The Jewish refugees cherished the freedom of movement, the opportunities for establishing a livelihood, and the comparatively greater security of their rights that they enjoyed in Prussia.

In all probability, Marion Samuel's Ueckermünde grandparents and great-grandparents were the type of Jewish immigrants whom the influential Second Reich historian Heinrich von Treitschke had caricatured as itinerant hawkers. "As immigration steadily increases, the question of how we can merge this foreign people with our own becomes more pressing," Treitschke thundered in a notorious 1879 address. "Year after year, a horde of eager trouser-selling youths presses over our eastern border from the inexhaustible Polish cradle, and their children and their children's children will eventually control the stock exchanges and the newspapers of Germany."[36] The Samuel family never rose that far.

In 1904, the Ueckermünde chronicler, reporting on the candidates for a teaching position in the apparently unattractive town, wrote: "Only one applicant, a Jew, responded to the announcement. As such, he was undesirable, and the city found itself in an awkward predicament."[37] Apart from such discrimination, though, the Protestant majority in Vorpommern, like that in Arnswalde's Neumark region, showed no militant enmity toward their Jewish fellow citizens through the early decades of the twentieth century.

As in Arnswalde, the synagogue in Ueckermünde was destroyed during the Kristallnacht attacks of November 9–10, 1938. While no documentation of the Arnswalde attacks exists, Ueckermünde provides us with an eyewitness account from Anni Buske, who was working as a gardener there at the time. According to Buske, "Around eleven o'clock on the morning of November 10, a middle school teacher stood with his students (all of them in uniform) in front of the apothecary. On his command, the students ran across the street with stones in their hands and threw them at the display window of the Daus Confectionery. I know this to be true," Buske adds, "because I was on my way to take flowers to a silver wedding and I heard the stones rattling over the market square. I went there and saw for myself what was happening."

On the same morning, an old Jew named August Senger was forced out of his residence, possibly by the same Jungvolk group led by the middle school teacher. (The Deutsches Jungvolk, or German Youth, was a branch of the Hitler Youth organization for boys ages ten to thirteen.) He was driven through the streets to the Schlossplatz, where books and Torah scrolls from the Jewish synagogue in the Töpferstrasse were being burned. Senger was ordered to read the Ten Commandments from the Torah scroll for the mob assembled there. "He was shaking so much from fear," Buske remembers, "that he could not read the commandments. He refused. They dragged him away."

A daughter of an Ueckermünde businessman named Rhein lingered to view the destruction of the plundered synagogue and was therefore late for lunch. Reportedly, "her father was angry over her thoughtless curiosity. He boxed her ears, for the first time in her life, and said heatedly: 'This time it is the Jews. Perhaps we Catholics are next!'" That response was an exception, but the way Kristallnacht unfolded in Ueckermünde does indicate that it was the work of a minority. It was carried out by a group of youths led by a committed National Socialist teacher, and accompanied only by a small contingent of the curious. Most citizens kept themselves in the background and looked away.

At around noon on November 10, the Jewish men of the town were forced to gather up the shattered pieces of glass and rubble. Edler von der Planitz, the acting president of the local government in the nearby city of Stettin, telegraphed Berlin that evening about the events in Ueckermünde: "The interior of the synagogue was demolished. The contents were removed and burned. . . . There was no looting. The display windows of two Jewish stores were broken. Six antique weapons and two new Teschings [small guns] were confiscated from Dr. Glaser, the Jewish former member of the national chamber of physicians. He surrendered them without objection."[38]

As far as I could ascertain, there are no relatives of Ernst Samuel living in Ueckermünde today. We can get a glimpse of his family's history, though, from their postwar application for restitution. Ernst's father, Adolf Samuel, was born in 1867 in Dobberschul in the Pyritz region and was married in 1894 in the town of Seelow in Oderbruch. For unknown reasons, he hanged himself in October 1926. His wife, Helene, died in 1931 or 1932. In addition to Ernst, they had five other children. There is very little that is documented about their lives.[39]

Ernst's oldest sibling, his sister Hildegard, was born on May 26, 1895. Following her school years in Ueckermünde, she attended Salomon's Business Academy in Berlin. She then completed an apprenticeship at Aronheim & Cohn, the large department store in Stettin. Soon after finishing the apprenticeship, Hildegard began a career as a buyer in Berlin, where she married Georg Cohn, a businessman. During the summer of 1937, the two of them emigrated through Copenhagen to São Paulo. They remained childless. In 1961, Hildegard and Georg Cohn moved to West Berlin.

Another sister, Margarethe, born on May 12, 1899, was murdered during the Holocaust in an unknown place at an unknown time.

Hans, a brother, was born on May 27, 1900. In 1928, he married Louise Schlegel in Berlin-Wilmersdorf. The two of them emigrated to Shanghai in 1939 or 1940. Hans Samuel died childless in Los Angeles in 1951.

Margot, Ernst's youngest sister, was born on December 1, 1908. In the 1920s she went to Berlin to work as a domestic, and in 1933 she moved from there to Amsterdam, where she married James S. Rosenthal. From 1941 to 1943, she was confined to the ghetto in Amsterdam. From 1943 to 1945, she endured the Vught, Auschwitz-Birkenau, Reichenbach, and Trautenau concentration camps. She was liberated at Porta Westfalica on April 29, 1945. Her husband did not survive. After a period of recovery in Sweden in 1945, Margot returned to the Netherlands. She emigrated to the United States in 1947, where she remarried, worked as a shoe saleswoman, and died, childless, in Los Angeles in August 1983.

Ernst's other brother, Kurt, was born on June 26, 1901, and later moved to Stettin. In 1928, he was married there to Grete

Hollywood,Calif.,den 28.Februar 1968

Ärztliches Gutachten

zum Antrag auf Entschädigung wegen Schadens an Körper oder Gesundheit
nach dem Bundesgesetz zur Entschädigung für die Opfer
der nationalsozialistischen Verfolgung

XXX/ der _Frau Margot Lewis_____, geb. am __1. Dezember 1908

wohnhaft in Los Angeles,California, 90057   126 South Coronado Street

Beruf: früher ___Haushaltsangestellte____ jetzt _Verkäuferin in einem Schuhwaren-
                                                                        geschäft.
(Legitimierung durch Personalpapiere erforderlich)

_____ U.S.Einbürgerungsurkunde No. 7172315

A. Vorgeschichte
(Nach Angaben des Antragstellers bei der Untersuchung)

I. Beruflicher Werdegang

Möglichst lückenlose Erfassung der Tätigkeiten vor, während und nach der Verfolgung bis
zur Gegenwart, in Stichworten:

Vor der Verfolgung - bis 1933 Haushaltsangestellte in Berlin.

Während der Verfolgung: bis zum Frühjahr 1933 - Haushaltsangestellte in Berlin,
von 1933 bis 1936 in Amsterdam (Holland) - Haushaltsangestell
Heiratete in 1936 einen Herrn James S.Rosenthal und war bis
1941 im eigenen Haushalt und im Geschäft ihres Ehemannes täti
Von 1941 bis März 1943 im Judénviertel in Amsterdam gelebt un
vielerlei Misshelligkeiten und Einschränkungen unterworfen gewesen.
Von März 1943 bis Mai 1945 in verschiedenen KZ-Lagern Zwangsarbeit verrichtet

Nach der Verfolgung: Von Mai 1945 bis August 1945 in Schweden zunächst in Kranken-
häusern,später in einem Erholungsheim versorgt worden.
Von August 1945 bis November 1947 in Amsterdam ohne Berufstätig-
keit,von Wohlfahrtsorganisationen unterstützt,gelebt.
Seit November 1947 in den USA und seit Januar 1948 in Los Angele
ansässig und bis 1952 verschiedene Stellungen als Verkäuferin be
kleidet;seit 1952 bis heute bei derselben Firma als Verkäuferin
in einem Schuhwarengeschäft angestellt.

II. Krankheitsvorgeschichte:

1. Familienvorgeschichte:
Vater litt an Diabetes und verübte 1926 Selbstmord.
Mutter in 1931 an Leberkrebs gestorben.
Zwei Brüder und eine Schwester durch n-s Gewaltmassnahmen umgekommen.
Der älteste Bruder starb 1951 im Alter von 51 Jahren an Herzschlag.
Eine ältere Schwester lebt in Berlin,ist herzleidend.

Der erste Ehemann der A'stn.ist durch n-s Gewaltmassnahmen umgekommen.

The first page of a physician's report submitted by Margot Lewis (b. Samuel) as part of the documentation for her case for restitution. See translation on next page. (*Landesentschädigungsamt Berlin*)

Registration No._____ Hollywood, Calif.   28 February 1968

Physician's Report
regarding an application for compensation for damage to body or health
according to the federal law concerning the victims of National Socialist persecution

Margot Lewis   born 1 December 1908
Currently resides: Los Angeles, California, 90057 126 South Coronado Street
Occupation, previous: Domestic   current: Clerk in shoe store

(Personal identification documents required for legitimization)
U.S. naturalization certificate No. 7172315

A. Previous history
(according to interview with applicant)

I. Career
Virtually complete history of employment before, during, and after the persecution until
the present, in summary:

Before the persecution: until 1933—domestic in Berlin.
During the persecution: until early 1933—domestic in Berlin.
  From 1933 until 1936—domestic in Amsterdam (Holland).
  In 1936, married Mr. James S. Rosenthal and was a housewife, and
  worked in her husband's business until 1941.
  From 1941 to March 1943, lived in the Jewish Quarter of
  Amsterdam and experienced much unpleasantness and many
  restrictions.
  From March 1943 until May 1945, performed forced labor in vari-
  ous concentration camps.

After the persecution: From May until August 1945, was initially in a hospital
  in Sweden, then cared for in a recovery home.
  From August 1945 to November 1947, lived in Amsterdam without
  employment and was supported by welfare organizations.
  Since November 1947, has been resident in the U.S.A., and since
  January 1948 in Los Angeles; until 1952 held various positions as a
  sales clerk; from 1952 to today has been employed by the same
  company, a shoe store.

II. History of illnesses:
  1. Family health history:
  Father suffered from diabetes and committed suicide in 1926.
  Mother died of lung cancer in 1931.
  Two brothers and a sister were killed by National Socialist violence.
  Eldest brother died of a heart attack in 1951 at the age of 51.
  An older sister who lives in Berlin suffers from heart disease.
  Her first husband was killed by National Socialist violence.

Schön, a Stettin native. In 1939 he lived at König-Albert-Strasse 39, and on February 12, 1940, he was deported (together with twelve hundred other Jews from the city) to Poland's Lublin district, on the eastern edge of the German area of occupation. According to information from Yad Vashem, the Israeli Holocaust archive, Kurt and Grete Samuel died on an unknown date in the town of Piaski, most probably as the result of forced labor, though possibly of disease resulting from the unhygienic conditions. A letter written in October 1941 by Max and Martha Buchwitz, who were also deported from Stettin to Piaski, lays out the scene: "There is much sorrow here, and never a ray of light. Elderly people, women in their prime, a blooming 21-year-old—no one can withstand the epidemic." In February 1942, the Buchwitzes wrote to their daughter: "From our family, no word. They cannot be far away, on the border near the Bug. Nothing but rumors! All that we can be sure of is that some of them are dead."[40]

Chapter 3

People Fall into a Hole

ERNST AND CILLY SAMUEL LEFT ARNSWALDE WITH THEIR four-year-old daughter in 1935, shortly after the town's Nazi sympathizers forced the W. A. Samuel store to close and the Samuels to sell the building.[41] The three of them moved to Berlin, where Cilly's older brother, Martin, and his family had settled in the 1920s. The other members of the family—Cilly's parents, Jenny and Carl, her brother Arthur, and perhaps also her youngest brother, Werner—moved to Königsberg, where Cilly's sister Helene had already settled some years earlier with her husband.[42]

The motivation for the moves was clear. In the anonymity of a large city, the persecuted felt in less danger of attack than in the smaller, more accessible provincial communities, which offered fewer opportunities for evasion. But while anonymity at first provided protection against daily discrimination, at the time of the deportations it became a deadly disadvantage—because the newly arrived lacked, as a rule, the contacts who could give timely warnings and make it possible to go into hiding.

After his arrival in Berlin, Ernst Samuel opened a cigar shop on Rhinower Strasse, in the Prenzlauer Berg district. The 1936 Berlin telephone directory lists the shop's number as D4-5222, but in the 1937 edition the listing is no longer to be found. The Berlin address directories for 1935 and 1936 have an entry for "Ernst Samuel, Cigar Shop, Rhinower Str. 11." In the address books from 1937 and 1938, though, Ernst Samuel is listed as a "staff salesman," indicating that he was no longer an independent shopkeeper. The 1939, 1940, and 1941 editions identify him only as a "salesman," from which it appears that he had by then also lost his employment. The Samuel family is not listed at all in the address directories from 1942 and 1943. Nevertheless, they were still alive, and, as the financial confiscation records of the Berlin-Brandenburg region attest, were living behind the narrow ground-floor shop at the front of the Rhinower Strasse building. Their apartment consisted of one room with a separate kitchen. The rent was thirty-five marks.[43]

The building belonged to Max Waschinsky and his wife, Wally, who lived on the second floor.[44] The Samuels' tiny apartment and the equally tiny cigar shop were to the right of the entrance. The building was populated almost exclusively by working-class families, among them a bailiff, a tax inspector, two drivers, and two postal inspectors. Today the building has been significantly renovated, but to this day a heavy iron grate hangs over the window facing the interior courtyard.

Marion Samuel entered first grade in the neighborhood public school on April 1, 1937. The school building stood at Sonnenburger Strasse 20, so Marion had to walk only about three hundred yards to get there.[45] On May 16, 1938, at the beginning of second grade—at that time in Berlin called the seventh—she was forced to leave that school, and was enrolled instead in the Third Public School of the Jewish community, located at Rykestrasse 53. However, that school was already filled beyond capacity, so Marion was apparently immediately transferred to the newly established Sixth Jewish Elementary School on Choriner Strasse.[46] (The sturdy brick building of the Jewish school on Rykestrasse still stands today; the building on Choriner Strasse was destroyed by bombing.)

For Marion Samuel, this must have been a comparatively happy

Marion Samuel's file card from the index of Jewish schoolgirls. Alongside her parents' names and addresses, the card records Marion's birth in 1931, inoculation in 1932, and her entire school career from her first school enrollment in April 1937 to her "withdrawal" from schooling on June 30, 1942. (Bundesarchiv Berlin, ZSg 138) time. For many of the Jewish students, whose parents had tried to become assimilated Germans, this was their first experience of an environment that was not determined by the Christian majority. They celebrated the Jewish holidays with their classmates, learned about Palestine, and enjoyed a life without racial discrimination. The school was also quite progressive, even if the students did not necessarily notice that fact. It was understood, for example, that students in their first year would not receive grades but would instead be given a verbal evaluation. Overall, the Jewish schools allowed the children considerable freedom, in marked contrast to the German public schools, which were run on a regimen of discipline and punishment.

"The students enrolled here did not think it peculiar that boys and girls were taught together, that there was no corporal punishment, and that they were not required to sit bolt upright with hands folded while attending to the teacher's every word," writes the historian Birgit Kirchhöfer about the Rykestrasse school. "The children who had transferred from the public schools immediately sensed the difference in the rules, and in their reminiscences noted how easy it was for them to fit into the new class. They no longer had the feeling of being outsiders; rather, they were each only one Jew among many."

In 1941, the Rykestrasse school building was confiscated for a German field post. From then on, the students were taught in various buildings still administered by the Jewish community. Elisabeth Siegel (b. 1929), who like Marion Samuel had to leave the German public school system in 1938 and enter a Jewish school, described the last months of that education: "The school wandered from place to place. We studied in the Auerbach Orphanage on Schönhauser Allee, then we were housed for a short time on Choriner Strasse, and finally we wound up on Kaiser Strasse. The teachers limited their lessons to what was possible to teach under such circumstances. We often studied until it was dark. We were told, 'Everything can be taken from you; only that which you have in your head is always yours.' "

Other details in Elisabeth Siegel's description show how her school sought to fortify its students against the ever more oppressive living conditions. "At the entrance of the Rykestrasse school there was a room where children whose parents were both working could eat. In the summer of 1941, our class joined the upper classes in taking responsibility for the care of the gravestones in the Jewish cemetery. The cemetery became a kind of vacation camp. We gathered early in the morning by the cemetery wall, where a kitchen had been set up for preparing warm meals. We worked with rakes until noon. We watered the flowers and cleared the paths. . . . When the first letters, or more often postcards, reached us from [the ghettoes in] Warsaw and Litzmannstadt [Lodz], our principal, Herr Sinasohn, collected the addresses. We went door to door to the homes of Jewish families to ask for money, flour, sugar, and tea. These items were made into small packages in Herr Sinasohn's office and labeled; then a group of students would go to different neighborhoods throughout the city and place the packages, marked 'Of no value,' in the mailboxes. At first we received thank-you letters. Later, most of the letters we sent out were returned to us, marked 'Addressee deceased' or 'Address unknown.' "[47]

Finally, in the summer of 1942, the right to attend school was taken from Jewish children. The official notice from the Reich Minister for Science, Education, and National Culture read: "In view of the recent development of Jewish settlements, the Reich Minister of the Interior (Reich Main Security Office), in cooperation with the

Reich Association of Jews in Germany, orders the closure of all Jewish schools by June 30, 1942, and declares that from July 1, 1942, onward, the instruction of Jewish children by paid or unpaid teachers is forbidden."[48] Because Marion could no longer go to school and her parents had now been enlisted as forced laborers, from this point forward she was often left to care for herself.

From April 1941, Marion's father was forced to work in the Daimler-Benz plant in Berlin-Marienfelde, where tanks and heavy train machinery were being produced. If one inquires today at the DaimlerChrysler archives about the Jewish forced laborers, one is treated with the same courtesy and efficiency as a person wishing to buy a new car. Within seconds, I received the following information: "Name: Samuel, Ernst Israel / Born Nov. 6 1905 / Nationality: Jew / Entered: April 3 1941 / Departed: March 17 1943 / Factory No. 33893 / Residence: Berlin N 58 Rhinower Str. 11." In the personnel book for the Marienfelde factory, one can see the original entry. The notation "Jew" appears in the space next to "control number" 257079; the space for "occupation" remains empty, while "unskilled worker" has been entered for the type of work. Each entry is followed by codes for the responsible social and medical insurance agencies. Ernst Samuel and his brother-in-law Martin worked in the same section at Daimler.[49] This is the only evidence that close contact was established between Ernst's and Martin's families in Berlin.

Daimler-Benz was required to pay Jewish forced laborers according to the pay scale for "unskilled labor." In principle, the Jewish worker was placed in class I, the lowest on the salary scale, but a significantly higher income tax was subtracted from a Jewish laborer's paycheck than from that of the "Aryan" workers. Ernst Samuel's weekly earnings were 52 Reichsmarks (RM), but his take-home pay was only 28 RM; the other 24 marks, withheld for taxes, flowed into the coffers of state and social welfare agencies.

In order to estimate the extent of exploitation by the state correctly, one should know that the additional state expenditures for a worker beyond his salary were barely more than 10 percent of his gross pay. Although the employer did contribute to the social insurance fund, Jews were refused all health and welfare benefits. And, of course, Jewish parents did not receive a child-care allocation. Just how much Daimler-Benz itself profited from a Jewish laborer is difficult to determine. It is clear, though, that some 46 percent of a Jewish worker's salary was expropriated and used to stabilize social networks that had been undermined by the war, all for the benefit of the majority "Aryan" population.

While Ernst was working at Daimler-Benz, Cilly Samuel was probably a forced laborer in the delivery facility of the Blaupunkt company on Hedemannstrasse. Her weekly take-home pay was twenty marks.[50] What life was like in Cilly's department cannot be

NEXT PAGE: List of Jews who performed forced labor producing tanks at the Daimler-Benz factory in Berlin-Marienfelde. The entries for Martin and Ernst Samuel are on the third and fourth lines from the bottom. From left to right, the columns on the left-hand page show the factory number, control number, worker's name, birthplace, marital status, birth date, occupation, and the start and end dates of the work. The columns on the right-hand page record when and where a "receipt card" was issued, the assorted "begin work" and "end work" dates on that card, the health insurance number, type of work, worker's residence, and miscellaneous comments. (*DaimlerChrysler AG, Konzernarchiv Stuttgart,* Personalbücher, *Werk Marienfelde*)

Fabrik-Nr.	Kontroll-Nr.	Vor- und Zuname des Arbeiters	Geburts-Ort und -Kreis	Familien-stand	Tag, Monat, Jahr der Geburt	Beruf des Arbeiters	Datum des Dienstantritts			Datum des Dienstaustritts		
							Tag	Monat	Jahr	Tag	Monat	Jahr
	Jude											
3385	257 083	Ignatz Israel Mathes	Berlin	verh.	16. V. 96	—	3.	IV.	41	17.	6.	42
	Jude											
886	257 076	Max Israel Neumann	Wien	verh.	11. 7. 92	—	3.	IV.	41	7.	6.	41
	Jude											
887	257 084	Georg Israel Prager	Berlin	verh.	11. II. 72	—	3.	IV.	41	14.	5.	41
	Jude											
888	257 085	Willi Israel Quitzow	Arnswalde	verh.	20. V. 85	—	3.	IV.	41	11.	3.	43
	Jude											
889	257 086	Siegfried Israel Reich	Berlin	ledig	21. II. 73	—	3.	IV.	41	17.	8.	42
	Jude											
890	257 088	Hans Israel Max Rund	Kolberg	verh.	18. III. 93	—	3.	IV.	41	17.	8.	42
	Jude											
891	257 087	Erich Israel Sachs	Berlin	ledig	16. VI. 00	—	3.	IV.	41	13.	1.	42
	Jude											
892	257 078	Gerh. Israel Saling	Sagan	ledig	2. III. 07	—	3.	IV.	41	18.	3.	43
	Jude											
893	257 079	Ernst Israel Samuel	Neckarmünde	verh.	6. II. 05	—	3.	IV.	41	18.	3.	43
	Jude											
894	257 080	Martin Israel Samuel	Arnswalde	verh.	8. V. 99	—	3.	IV.	41	25.	2.	43
	Jude											
895	257 089	Willy Israel Schlesinger	Stuttgart	verh.	28. V. 07	—	3.	IV.	41	10.	3.	43
	Jude											
896	257 090	Georg Israel Sollochoff	Charlott.	verh.	14. VIII. 07	—	3.	IV.	41	17.	6.	42

Nummer und Vers.-Anstalt	Ausstellungsort	Der Ausstellung			Die Quittungskarte war mit wieviel Marken versehen?		Nummer des Krankenkassenbuches		Beschäftigt in Werkstatt?	Wohnung des Arbeiters	Bemerkungen
		Tag	Monat	Jahr	Beim Dienst-Antritt	Beim Dienst-Austritt					
3	A. O. K.								257	Bln. N 54,	40/a 8m100 25 b
Bln.	Bln.	2	9	40			262	514	Hilfsarbeiter	Lothringerstr. 57	St. K.
1	174. Pol. Rev.								257	Bln. N. 30	40/a 917 524 25 b
Bln.	Bln.	2.	III.	41			263	213	Hilfsarbeiter	Schönhauserstr.	St. K.
1	127. Pol. Rev.								257	Charlottenburg	25 On 40/528 139 23 b
Bln.	Berlin	17	III.	41			264	181	Hilfsarbeiter	Mühlstr. 3	St. K.
1	82. Pol. Rev.								257	Berlin O.	40/a 917 074 28 b
Bln.	Bln.	22	III.	41			265	1450	Hilfsarbeiter	Rüdersdorfer str. 30	St. K.
							266	1089	257 Hilfsarbeiter	Bln. N. 35 Rheinsbergerstr. 30	40/a 917 513 23 b St. K.
1	170. Pol. Rev.								257	Bln. N. 50	40/a 802 965 23 b
Bln.	Bln.	11.	III.	39			267	1090	Hilfsarbeiter	Neue Ansbacherstr.	St. K.
1	148. Pol. Rev.								257	Halensee	8 40/a 911 453 23 b
Bln.	Bln.	15	III.	39			268	26	Hilfsarbeiter	Joach. Friedrichstr.	St. K.
1	A. O. K. Bln.								257	Bln. O. 2.	48 40/a 916 194 23 b
Bln.	Reg. d. f. A. K.	17.	III.	40			269	1472	Hilfsarbeiter	Alexanderstr.	St. K.
1	63. Pol. Rev.								257	Bln. N 58,	37 B. 40/486 670 h. 23 b
Bln.	Bln.	18.	III.	40			270	1473	Hilfsarbeiter	Rheinsbergerstr. 11	St. K.
	A. O. K. Bln.	11.	III.	41			271	1392	257 Hilfsarbeiter	Bln. N. 35, Barbarossastr.	40/163 1615 h. 23 b 45 St. K.
	243. Reg. 44. Wilmersdf.	2	III.	41			272	1456	257 Hilfsarbeiter	Wilmersdorf Günzelstr. 10	P 41/437 56 23 b St. K.
	A. O. K. Bln. Trier H. 3	4. 11.	III. III.	41 39			273	576	257 Hilfsarbeiter	Bln. N. 4, Ackerstr. 173	F. 41/1468 28 b St. K.

determined in any detail, but Camilla Neumann, a forced laborer in another department at Blaupunkt, describes her experience:

> I arrived at Blaupunkt as a factory worker. We had four supervisors, two male and two female. One of the male overseers, Schindler, appeared to behave correctly, but was dishonest and dangerous. The other, a Dutchman by the name of van Geest, spoke to us only as the work necessitated, and had anyone who did not please him delivered to the Gestapo. One of the women overseers was decent, but the other was arrogant and would have fit in well as a guard in a concentration camp.
>
> My colleagues belonged to all classes of society. They ranged in age from sixteen to sixty years old. We were not supposed to know what we were producing, but we discovered that we were assembling listening equipment for the Wehrmacht, to be used in airplanes. After six weeks of training, I became a reel winder. We had to make thirty-two reels each day—not right away on our first day, but each day we worked we had to make more and more. At one point, when I had reached twenty-eight reels a day, the Wehrmacht came back and returned many of the listening devices as unusable. The devices were disassembled, and they found that the problem lay with the reels. From the control numbers, it could be determined who had made the defective reels, and the four workers identified as responsible were sent to the Gestapo. There they received a warning and were told that if this happened again, they would be sent to a concentration camp. Since these were the best workers, I became very anxious and didn't want to do this kind of work. I no longer even tried to finish thirty-two reels, and insisted that I could not carry such a workload.
>
> Because of this, I was transferred to another section. The work here did not entail such responsibility, and I could fill my quota. Men and women worked together here in the same hall. I sat in a corner among only academics. They were very nice people, and although we were all very unhappy, we often joked with one anoth-

er. As soon as the overseers turned their backs, we ignored the rules against talking.

As I have already mentioned, van Geest sent many women to the Gestapo. Among the older women, we had some unfortunate people— sick and suffering and therefore not exactly skilled. They had to clean toilets and perform other unpleasant tasks. If he didn't like them, he had them taken away. He claimed that one of the other women had made advances toward him, and although he was extremely handsome, none of us believed it. She disappeared and we could not ask her about it. There was also a homosexual woman. For months, van Geest didn't know about her, but as soon as he found out she too disappeared.

After she narrowly avoided arrest at the beginning of 1943, Camilla Neumann approached her supervisor. "I explained to van Geest what had happened, and asked him if I might lodge a complaint. He said that there was nothing he could do, that I should go to the personnel office in Schmargendorf. I will never forget how badly I was treated by the head of the office. He replied with a cold laugh: 'If the state has decided upon your "removal," I will do nothing to hinder it. I am no enemy of the state.' I turned and went away without a word."[51]

On Saturday, February 27, 1943, Ernst, Cilly, and Marion were arrested. The arrest occurred as part of a larger roundup, which the Reich Main Security Office had ordered to be carried out abruptly at the beginning of the workday. The roundup was aimed at the "armaments Jews" and their families. Later, it became known as the Factory Action.

Joseph Goebbels, the Gauleiter (Nazi party district leader) of Berlin, had written in mid-February that "by the February 28 deadline," the Berlin Jews would be "rounded up into camps and then deported, in batches of two thousand per day." Two days later, the Reich Main Security Office issued "guidelines for the technical realization" of Goebbels's order, not only for Berlin but for the entire Reich. With the help of officials from the Abwehr (German military intelligence) and the security officers of individual firms, the Gestapo carried out a survey of all the Jews working in private concerns, proceeding "as unobtrusively as possible" and using information supplied in advance by the responsible employment bureaus.

On the morning of February 27, Berlin police stations were ordered to initiate their part of the large-scale action. The Jews in the factories, as well as all the Jews on the street, easily recognizable because of their star-shaped badges, were to be picked up and delivered to designated assembly points: the Jewish community building on Grosse Hamburger Strasse, the Clou ballroom, and a pair of barracks. Of the eleven thousand potential victims, seven thousand were seized.

It is quite remarkable that four thousand already stigmatized and socially isolated men and women were able to escape a major raid organized largely in secret. In the middle of the war, at a time of sweeping anti-Jewish hatred, German citizens, administrators, armament inspectors, "Aryan" overseers, policemen, and, in one case, even a member of the SS, warned the persecuted.[52] The Samuels, however, were not among those so alerted. Just as planned by the organizers of the roundup, they fell one by one into the clutches of the police and the SS. Ernst Samuel was picked up at the Daimler-Benz factory, his wife was arrested at Blaupunkt, and their eleven-year-old daughter, Marion, was taken from their home. They were led away by the police or by staffers of the Reich Association of Jews in Germany.

The Reich Association was a compulsory organization that coordinated the affairs of the Jews, and did so under the close supervision of the authorities and within ever-tightening restrictions. The Blaupunkt worker Camilla Neumann, whose husband, Ludwig, was arrested, removed her star and inquired about him in front of the assembly point at Grosse Hamburger Strasse. She writes in her memoir:

> What I gleaned in bits and pieces from various people was shocking. Since their arrest, the Jews had received no food. It was simply no longer possible for the Jewish community to provide for these thousands of people, and for those rounded up to receive even the smallest things. The transports were to begin that evening, on March 1, leaving one after another. . . . Married couples never saw each other again because they had worked in different factories. Parents never saw their children again. Children were taken from their homes and deported in separate transports. It was all so shattering, and the terrible winter cold made it even worse.[53]

Ernst and Cilly Samuel were taken to different collection points and so did not see each other again after they were arrested. Cilly was deported to Auschwitz on March 1, in the thirty-first Jewish transport from Berlin. Ernst followed two days later in Transport 33. Both of them were required to fill out lengthy property declarations at the time of their arrests, demanding information such as whether any relatives had emigrated and where they had gone. (Cilly Samuel wrote, "Mother, three brothers, one of them to USA.") Under the heading "liquid assets," Ernst Samuel wrote, "approx. 2 mk." Because the arrest happened on a Saturday morning, he also specified the expected amount of his next paycheck: "approx. 50 mk. gross." For "total amount of current assets," he wrote the sum of "approx. 52 mk."

Vermögenserklärung

Vornamen (Rufname unterstreichen) und Zuname (bei Ehefrauen auch Mädchenname): _____

Beruf: _____ Jude? _____

Letzte Beschäftigung (Firma, Gehalt, Lohn): _____

Wohnung (Stadt, Stadtteil, Straße und Hausnummer, seit wann? _____

Name, Anschrift und evtl. jüdische Rassezugehörigkeit des Hauseigentümers: _____

Größe der Wohnung (Zimmerzahl und -art, WC, Warmwasser, Dampf- oder Warmwasserheizung, Balkon, Wohngeschoß, Fahrstuhl, Gartenbenutzung, Nebenräume wie Diele, Badezimmer, Mädchenkammer, Keller, Boden usw. Genaue Angaben): _____

Höhe der monatlichen oder vierteljährlichen usw. Miete (Mietvertrag beifügen): _____

Sind Sie Untermieter? (Dann auch Name, Anschrift und evtl. jüdische Rassezugehörigkeit des Untervermieters angeben): _____

The first page of the sixteen-page property declaration form that Ernst Samuel was required to fill out after his arrest on February 28, 1943. The notation "IV/471" in the upper right-hand corner denotes the number of

Attention!

Matters that are being carried forward in accordance with a previous arrangement are not to be entered here. An individual form must be filled out for each person (including wives and children). For minor children and wives the form should normally be filled out by the legal representative (father) or the husband. This is also the case when the wife or child do not receive an income or possess any property. Stock certificates, contracts, and other documentation of investments are to be submitted with the completed form.

IV/471

Property Declaration

First names (underline the name by which you are called) and last name (for women, include the maiden name):

Ernst Israel Samuel

Occupation: *Laborer* Jew? *Yes*

Current employment (company, pay, wages):

Daimler-Benz Marienfelde

Residence (city, section, street and house number, since when?):

N. 58 Rhinowerstr. 11

Name, address, and degree of Jewish racial identity of landlord:

Max Waschinsky, Rhinowerstr. 11

Size of the residence (number and type of rooms, toilet, hot water, steam heat, balcony, floor in building, elevator, use of garden, additional rooms such as entrance hall, bathroom, maid's room, cellar, grounds, etc. Give detailed description):

1 Room and Kitchen

Amount of monthly or quarterly rent (submit copy of lease): *35 marks*

Do you have a boarder? (If so, give name, address, and degree of Jewish racial identity of the boarder): *No*

the collection point and of the arrestee. The handwritten number at the bottom of the first page was added by the Berlin-Brandenburg tax office. See translation above. (*Brandenburgerisches Landeshauptarchiv*)

Mein gesamtes Vermögen im In- und Ausland
setzt sich (in Reichsmark) folgendermaßen zusammen:

A. Aktiven:

I. Flüssiges Vermögen:

1. Bargeldbestand (Höhe und Aufbewahrungsort): _Ca. 2.- RM_

2. Guthaben bei Geldinstituten:

Anstalt	Kontobezeichnung	Kto.-Nr.	Betrag
a) inländische			
b) ausländische			

(Bei Sparbüchern sind der Verwahrungsort und evtl. Kenn- oder Losüngsworte anzuführen.)

3. Wertpapiere (Anleihen, Aktien, Kuxe, Lose, Wechsel usw.):

Bezeichnung	Stückzahl	Nennbetrag	Verwahrungsort *)	Bemerkung

*) Geldanstalt und Depotbezeichnung sind genau anzuführen.

4. Besitzen Sie ein Panzerschließfach und was befindet sich darin? (Anstalt, Nummer und evtl. Losungswort sind anzugeben): _____

The beginning of the main section of Ernst Samuel's property declaration form. See translation on next page. (*Brandenburgerisches Landeshauptarchiv*)

My entire property, in the country
and abroad (in Reichsmarks), consists of:

A. Investments and Income

I. Liquid property:

1. Cash (amount and storage location): *ca. 2 marks*

2. Bank balance

Bank	Account type	Account number	Balance
a) In the country			
b) Abroad			

(Enter location of passbook and any identification or passwords.)

3. Securities (loans, stocks, mining rights, lottery tickets, bills of
exchange, etc.)

Designation	Quantity	Nominal value	Storage location*	Comments

*Enter exact financial institution and designation.

4. Do you possess a safe, and what is to be found inside?
(Enter institution, number, and estimated worth.)

4. Haben Sie Anspruch auf Gehalt, Provisionen, Pensionen, Renten oder Vertragsabfertigungen?

Lohn ca 50,- brutto

5. Waren oder sind Sie pensionsversichert, sozialversichert? Bei welchen Anstalten und unter welcher Nummer?

6. Haben Sie Kautionen erlegt, bei wem und in welcher Höhe?

Betrag 10,- Mk
Betrag 10,- Mk

7. Ist Ihnen eine Erbschaft oder ein Vermächtnis angefallen? (Name des Erblassers, ungef. Wert und Nachlaß-
gericht angeben!)

8. Stehen Ihnen Nießbrauchrechte oder Ausgedinge zu? An welchen Sachen und in welchem Umfange?

9. Welche Ansprüche stehen Ihnen aus Lizenzverträgen, Patent-, Urheber-, Marken- und Musterschutzrechten usw.
zu?

10. Stehen Ihnen Unterhaltsansprüche zu? Gegen wen, aus welchem Grund und in welcher Höhe?

11. Stehen Ihnen Anwartschaftsrechte zu?

For Marion Samuel, these must have been dreadful days and nights. She was completely alone, without any relatives. Her name was on the list for Transport 32, which left for Auschwitz on March 2, but it was crossed out and placed instead on the list for the transport leaving the day after that. On March 1, after almost three full days of separation from her family, Marion was transferred from the Grosse Hamburger Strasse building to the collection point where her father was being held. Because Ernst Samuel filled out Marion's property declaration form, we know that they were reunited at this collection point, and that she did not make her final trip alone.

The Samuel family's apartment was sealed, and at first stood empty. Ten weeks after their deportation, a court executor prepared an inventory of its contents. He assigned a value of fifteen marks to the linens, three marks to the porcelain and kitchen uten-

OPPOSITE AND NEXT PAGES: Three of the subsequent pages from Ernst Samuel's property declaration form. The questions read:

4. Do you have a claim to salary, commissions, pensions, or contractual agreements?
    Wages ca. 50 marks gross
5. Do you have a vested pension or social insurance? With which institution and under what number?
6. Do you have security deposits? With whom and in what amount?
    Bewag [electric company]—*10 marks*
    Gasag [gas company]—*10 marks*
7. Have your received an inheritance or legacy? (Enter name of the deceased, amount, and name of probate court)
8. Do you have any hereditary usufructuary rights or expenditures? To which property and to what extent?
9. What claims do you have on licenses, patent rights, author rights, trademarks, registered designs, etc.?
10. Do you have any claims to maintenance? Against whom, on what grounds, and in what amount?
11. Do you have any claims on expectancies?

VI. Kunst- und Wertgegenstände:

Besitzen Sie Gemälde, Antiquitäten, Gold- oder Silberwaren, Schmuck, Juwelen oder sonstige Kunstgegenstände und Sammlungen? (Briefmarken, Münzensammlungen usw.) Stückzahl und ungefähr Wert sind anzugeben. Wo sind diese verwahrt? Der Depotschein ist beizufügen.

VII. Sind Ihnen gehörige Sachen bei anderen in Verwahrung? Name, Anschrift des Verwahrers sowie genaue Beschreibung und ungefähr Wert der Sachen sind anzuführen:

VIII. Liegen Eigentumsbeschränkungen (Eigentumsvorbehalte, Pfandrechte usw.) an einzelnen Vermögensteilen vor? Besitzen Sie sonstiges Vermögen, welches oben nicht angeführt ist?

IX. Höhe des jetzigen Gesamtvermögens (ohne Abzug der Passiven):

B. Passiven:

(Bei sämtlichen Schulden sind Name, evtl. jüdische Rassezugehörigkeit und Anschrift des Gläubigers, der Grund der Schuldverpflichtung, ihre Entstehungszeit, Höhe, Fälligkeit und Namen von Zeugen genau anzuführen. Schuldurkunden, Korrespondenzen und Urteile sowie sonstiges Beweismaterial sind beizulegen.)

I. Welche Schulden und Verpflichtungen haben Sie?

a) Aus Unternehmungen und Beteiligung an Unternehmungen?

sils, and one mark apiece to two flower tables. The child's chair, he noted, was "worthless." The couch, a metal bedstead, a wardrobe, and a round table and chairs were assigned somewhat higher values. In the Berlin telephone book from 1942, one can find the listing for the man who had evaluated everything so punctiliously: "Wilhelm Vesper Ob.-Ger.-Vollz., 55 Prenzlauer Allee 40534636."

All furniture, cutlery, duvets, and linens were sent to a specially authorized secondhand merchant. There, bombed-out Berliners with the proper vouchers could refurnish their homes. The NSV (National Socialist People's Welfare organization) also filled out its stocks with items left behind by those who had been deported, to provide care for German pensioners and the needy. The Reich Finance Ministry bureaucrats requested that the municipal adminis-

OPPOSITE:

VI. Art and Items of Value
Do you own any paintings, antiques, gold or silverware, jewelry, precious stones, or other such art items and collections? (Stamps, coins, etc.) Enter the quantity and approximate value. Where are they stored? Submit deposit receipt with completed form.

VII. Are any of your possessions being cared for by someone else? Enter their name, address, and an exact description and approximate value of the items.

VIII. Are there any claims or liens on any items of your property (retentions of title, pawn brokerage pledges, etc.)? Do you possess any other property that has not been entered above?

IX. Total amount of the aforementioned property (without subtracting liabilities):
    ca. 52 marks

B. Liabilities:
(For all debts, enter the name, Jewish racial identity, and address of the creditor. Specify the reason for the debt, the repayment terms, amount, maturity date, and the names of the witnesses. Submit all loan agreements, correspondence, judgments, and all pertinent evidence with the completed form.)

What debts and other financial responsibilities do you have?
    a) For business ventures and stakes in businesses?

VII. Haben Sie sonstige Verpflichtungen oder Passiven?

VIII. Höhe der gesamten Passiven:

IX. Höhe des jetzigen Gesamtvermögens (nach Abzug der Passiven):

Haben Sie jemanden die Vertretungsbefugnis (Vollmacht) erteilt? (Name, evtl. jüdische Rassezugehörigkeit und Anschrift des Vertretungsberechtigten sowie Umfang der Vertretungsbefugnis.)

Verschiedenes:

tration carefully carry out the sale of Jewish property to ensure that the items, "especially textiles and furnishings," "make it into the right hands"—such as of "those who had been bombed out, the newly married, the dependents of soldiers, etc." If the deported had possessed an especially well-appointed middle-class household, antique dealers and antiquarians took part in the liquidation of the property. Typically, however, a "court executor or some other reliable assessor—representatives of the municipal pawn shops proved valuable—determined the worth of individual items." Great care was taken to ensure that "nothing was given away."[54]

A clerk who worked in a shop run by Max Bier, a secondhand merchant in Berlin, remembers: "In September 1942, Herr Bier received a communication from the authorities containing a list of property in a 'Jewish estate' that Bier was to clear away by a certain date. . . . Anything that could be sold, even the nightgowns, was assessed, and the recommended price recorded. The hard-earned funds I had at my disposal just covered the price of a bookcase. It cost sixty marks, quite a bit of money for a schoolboy at that time; but there it stood in my room, and I immediately dubbed it 'the Jewish bookcase.' The aroma of powder still lingered in the drawer."

OPPOSITE:

VII. Do you have any other financial commitments?

VIII. Total amount of liabilities:

IX. Value of all property (minus liabilities):
   ca. 52 marks

Have you given anyone power of attorney? (Specify name and degree of Jewish racial identity. Provide a copy of the agreement and an explanation of the extent of the power.)

Miscellaneous:

— 16 —

Ich erkläre ausdrücklich, daß ich meine vorstehenden Angaben nach bestem Wissen gemacht und dabei insbesondere keinerlei Vermögenswerte verschwiegen habe. Ich versichere weiterhin, außer für meine Ehefrau und meine Kinder, deren Vermögen ich besonders angegeben habe, für andere Personen nur solche Vermögenswerte zu verwalten oder in Gewahrsam zu haben, die von mir ausdrücklich in dieser Vermögenserklärung (falls nicht anderweitig, in der letzten Spalte unter Verschiedenes) als fremde bezeichnet worden sind. Ich bin mir bewußt, daß falsche oder unvollständige Angaben geahndet werden.

Berlin , den 25/2. 43

_____
(Unterschrift)

The expropriation process produced revenue for the German state; at the same time, it allowed the political leadership to offer on the market the kind of goods that could hardly be produced during the war. The unpleasant shortages that were felt ever more acutely as the war progressed, and stimulated latent public dissatisfaction, could be selectively overcome. The only requirement was that the furnishings of some hundreds of thousands of western European Jewish homes be systematically brought to Germany for the benefit of bombed-out families.[55]

The total inventory of the Samuel family possessions was valued at 220 marks. After subtracting all the fees and the cost of the family's own deportation, 198 marks (roughly equivalent to $2,000 today) remained for deposit in the treasury of the German Reich. In addition, a total of 6.28 marks was returned from the Samuels' security deposit by the Berlin Electric Company—which had already developed form number DIN-A5, titled "Notification Concerning Evacuated Jews," for such cases—and 2.01 marks came from the municipal gas company. A final paycheck, for 11.08 marks, was also received from Blaupunkt. In all, the state took in 217.37 RM.

Unlike Blaupunkt, Daimler-Benz did not explicitly send to the

OPPOSITE: The final page of Ernst Samuel's property declaration form. The text reads:

I certify that I have made this declaration to the best of my ability and that I have not concealed any property. Furthermore, I guarantee that, except for the property of my wife and children, which I have listed separately, no other property of mine is being administered or held in trust by another person other than as noted on this form. I understand that giving false or incomplete information is punishable by law.

Berlin, 28 February 1943
Ernst Israel Samuel
(Signature)

Vermögenserklärung

Vornamen (Rufname unterstreichen) und Zuname (bei Ehefrauen auch Mädchenname):

Beruf: _____ Jude? _____

Letzte Beschäftigung (Firma, Gehalt, Lohn):

Wohnung (Stadt, Stadtteil, Straße und Hausnummer, seit wann?

Name, Anschrift und evtl. jüdische Rassezugehörigkeit des Hauseigentümers:

Größe der Wohnung (Zimmerzahl und -art, WC, Warmwasser, Dampf- oder Warmwasserheizung, Balkon, Wohngeschoß, Fahrstuhl, Gartenbenutzung, Nebenräume wie Diele, Badezimmer, Mädchenkammer, Keller, Boden usw. Genaue Angaben):

Höhe der monatlichen oder vierteljährlichen usw. Miete (Mietvertrag beifügen):

Sind Sie Untermieter? (Dann auch Name, Anschrift und evtl. jüdische Rassezugehörigkeit des Untervermieters angeben):

The first page of the property declaration for Marion Samuel, which her father filled out for her when they were reunited at collection point IV. In the upper right-hand corner, next to Marion's number, is the notation that she was previously held at "Gr[osse] Hamburger Str." Underneath that an official has written "son," crossed it out, and written "daughter." *(Brandenburgisches Landeshauptarchiv)* government the back wages owed to individual deported laborers. Daimler-Benz's bookkeeping department and the tax authorities had agreed on an alternative method. In the personnel records of the company's Berlin-Marienfelde branch, there are curious entries that claim that Ernst Samuel and the other Jewish forced laborers deported on February 27 continued to be employed at the factory until March 17. Thus, instead of directly passing the deportees' back wages to the government—a rather awkward bit of bookkeeping—Daimler-Benz sent the money to the state in the form of tax deductions that simply continued for two and a half weeks as if the deportations had not happened. This deal must have been struck sometime after February 8, the date when Martin Samuel was arrested: the Daimler-Benz personnel book had originally listed the end of Martin's service correctly, as February 8, but that was crossed out and replaced with a date of February 25 instead.[56]

The dispossession process continued until September 1943, and during this entire time the Samuels' apartment remained sealed. The finance office therefore had to continue to pay rent to Wally Waschinsky, the building's landlady, which totaled 245 marks. Since the liquidation of the household and Cilly's back wages had yielded only 217.37 marks, the German state sustained a fiscal loss of 27.63 RM.[57] All things considered, that was an exception.

Even in this case, though, the deportation of a pair of Jewish forced laborers and their child proved beneficial for the wartime economy. The Berlin "armaments Jews" were replaced by eastern European forced laborers. As the documents of the Reich Commissariat for the Security of the German People make clear, these forced laborers were brought to Berlin without their elderly and their children, without anyone who was feeble or ill. Since the Poles were young, they were separated by gender so they would not

641	Becker geb. Sonnenberg	Gerda Sara	24.8.14
642	Becker	Denny	19.2.41
643	Berelowski geb. Weis	Regina	12.9.14
644	Herzfeld geb. Becker	Selma Sara	13.12.97
645	Kaiser	Ilse Sara	30.12.23
646	Salinger geb. Ginsberg	Rosa Sara	19.8.93
647	Wilde	Heinz Israel	25.2.05
648	Schreiber geb. Sohn	Alice Sara	30.5.96
649	Brandt	Siegfried Israel	3.5.93
650	Reimann geb. Wilczinski	Erna Sara	19.7.91
651	Oppenstein	Ludwig Israel	18.8.90
~~652~~			
653	Böhm geb. Berndt	Frieda Sara	9.12.92
~~654~~			
655	Samuel	Gertrud Sara	25.11.89
656	Herzfeld	Max Israel	20.7.75
657	Herzfeld geb. Zucker	Jenny Sara	19.2.86
~~658~~			
659	Held geb. Littwack	Henny Sara	6.9.92
660	Loebel	Selma Sara	18.12.97

The list of Jews deported from Berlin to Auschwitz on Transport 32, which departed on March 2, 1943. Marion Samuel's name is at line 652; it was crossed off, and she was instead deported together with her father a day later. In the far right column is the number of her property declaration. (*Brandenburgerisches Landeshauptarchiv*)

Berlin	NO 55. Greifswalderstr. 20	III/1140
Berlin	dto	III/1141
Berlin	SW 68. Alexandrinenstr. 116	III/1142
Berlin	Charlbg. Uhlandstr. 194	III/1143
Berlin	NO 55. Filkezstr. 1	III/1144
Warschau	O.2.Rosenthalerstr. 39	III/1145
Berlin	Charlbg. Bleibtreustr. 41	III/1146
Kurz	Charl. Sybelstr. 56	III/1147
Berlin	W.62. Ale ststr. 35	III/1148
Gnesen	SO 36. Adalbertstr. 7	III/1149
Schönlanke	Charl. 4. Wielandstr. 44	III/1150
		III/1151
Stargardt	Charlbg. Wielandst. 37	III/1152
		III/1153
Kurz	Charlbg. Sybelstr. 56	III/1154
Gr. Trohlitz	Charlbg. Bleibtreustr. 41	III/1155
Odessa	Charlb . Bleib reustr. 41	III/1156
		III/1157
Ortelsburg	Charlbg. Agomisenstr. 22	III/1158
Grünheide	Charlbg. Wielandsb. 37	III/1159

Geheim- Staatspolizei
Staatspo ;,eileitstelle Berlin.

Berlin C 2
Grunerstraße 12
, den 1. Feb. 1943

Verfügung

Auf Grund des § 1 des Gesetzes über die Einziehung kommunistischen Vermögens vom 26. Mai 1933 — RGBl. I S. 293 — in Verbindung mit dem Gesetz über die Einziehung volks- und staatsfeindlichen Vermögens vom 14. Juli 1933 — RGBl. I S. 479 —, der Verordnung über die Einziehung volks- und staatsfeindlichen Vermögens im Lande Österreich vom 18. 11. 1938 — RGBl. I S. 1620 —, der Verordnung über die Einziehung volks- und staatsfeindlichen Vermögens in den sudetendeutschen Gebieten vom 12. 5. 1939 — RGBl. I S. 911 — und der Verordnung über die Einziehung von Vermögen im Protektorat Böhmen und Mähren vom 4. Oktober 1939 — RGBl. I S. 1998 — wird in Verbindung mit dem Erlaß des Führers und Reichskanzlers über die Verwertung des eingezogenen Vermögens von Reichsfeinden vom 29. Mai 1941 — RGBl. I S. 303 —

das gesamte Vermögen des — der   Ernst Israel Samuel

geborene   geboren am 6. 11. 05

in   Ueckermünde /Pomm.

zuletzt wohnhaft in   N 58, Rhinower -

Straße/Platz Nr.   11 vorn Ptr.

zugunsten des Deutschen Reiches eingezogen.

Im Auftrage

Wenden!

The Gestapo decree concerning the expropriation of Ernst Samuel's property. The decree is stamped "February 1, 1943": the officials forgot to reset the date stamp from February to March. See translation on next page. *(Brandenburgerisches Landeshauptarchiv)*

Decree

According to the Law Concerning the Confiscation of Communist Property, 26 May 1933 (RGBl. I, page 293); the Law Concerning the Confiscation of the Property of the Enemies of the People and the State, 14 July 1933 (RGBl. I, page 479); the Law Concerning the Confiscation of the Property of the Enemies of the People and the State in Austria, 18 November 1938 (RGBl. I, page 1620); the Law Concerning the Confiscation of the Property of the Enemies of the People and the State in Southern German areas, 12 May 1939 (RGBl. I, page 911); the Regulation Concerning the Confiscation of the Property of the Enemies of the People and the State in the Protectorate of Bohemia and Moravia, 4 October 1939 (RGBl. I, page 1993); and the Decree of the Führer and Reich Chancellor Concerning the Utilization of Confiscated Property of the Enemies of the Reich, 29 May 1941 (RGBl. I, page 303):

The entire property of *Ernst Israel Samuel*

born *6 November 1905*

in *Ueckermünde / Pomerania*

last resident at *Nr. 58, Rhinowerstr.*

street number: *11, front*

has been confiscated for the benefit of the state.

By order of

(Signature)

Zustellungs-Urkunde

Ausfertigung umstehenden Schriftstücks nebst einer beglaubigten Abschrift dieser Zustellungsurkunde habe ich heute im Auftrage der Geheimen Staatspolizei — Staatspolizeileitstelle Berlin — zum Zwecke der Zustellung an

d _____

_____

dem Empfänger selbst _____

_____

übergeben.

Berlin, den _____ 1943

Obergerichtsvollzieher in Berlin

D.R. Nr. _____

Beglaubigt:

Obergerichtsvollzieher

The reverse side of the Gestapo decree, with a "record of delivery" signed by the Executor of the Upper Court in Berlin, alleging that Ernst Samuel had received notice of the expropriation of his property. The text reads: "In the service of the Secret State Police (Berlin State Police Station), I have today given this completed documentation, together with a notarized copy of this delivery record, to the receiver himself."

conceive any children—clearly to the advantage of German demography. Moreover, the Polish workers were housed in barracks, leaving the homes and furnishings of Jews available for "Aryan" Germans.

As the Jews were deported, Poles from the Zamosc region, east of the city of Lublin, were brought to Berlin to replace them. In their place, a commission working under Heinrich Himmler's direction in the winter of 1942–43 began to settle ethnic Germans from Romania and Bosnia in the middle of the Polish heartland. Since the fall of 1940, these Germans had been stuck in camps, awaiting their promised farmsteads and growing more and more dissatisfied every day. The "armament Jews" were deported in the very same trains that brought the Polish forced laborers to Berlin. Camilla Neumann writes in her account of the Factory Action: "I saw what was happening around me and made my own conclusions. Thousands of men and women arrived in Berlin and were placed where the Jews once worked. I knew that our days were numbered."[58]

The Jews rounded up in the Factory Action, labeled as "unproductive dependents" in the Nazi parlance, were sent to Auschwitz—Marion Samuel among them.[59] Cattle cars stood ready for the deportees in the freight depot of the Berlin-Moabit train station near the Putlitz bridge. SS members and ordinary Berlin policemen ferried those destined for deportation in trucks to the loading platform. Because she was more than ten years old, Marion Samuel's deportation cost six and a half Reich pennies per mile, the same price as that for an adult traveling third class at the group rate. In fact, for the entire group of deportees, there was only a single one-way group ticket to Auschwitz.

Zur Beachtung!

Zwischen dem Oberfinanzpräsidenten Berlin-Brandenburg und
dem Oberbürgermeister der Reichshauptstadt Berlin ist ver-
einbart worden, daß bei der Bewertung der zu schätzenden
Sachen ein vernünftiger mittlerer Preis auf der Grundlage des
Vorkriegspreisniveaus, und zwar unter Berücksichtigung des
allgemeinen **Vorkriegsverkehrswertes** der Sachen gelten soll.

Akt.-Z. d. OFP

lt. Straßenliste 45 / 27 68

Schätzungsblatt Nr. 1

(Gehören zu einer Wohnung mehrere Schätzungs-
blätter, so sind diese laufend zu numerieren.)

Berlin- N 56 Straße: Rhinowerstr. Nr. 11 Lage: D 2.

Früherer Mieter bzw. Untermieter: Cilly Sara Samuel
(Früherer Eigentümer der Gegenstände)

Ungezieferfrei! — Nicht ungezieferfrei!
(Nichtzutreffendes bitte zu streichen!)

Schlüssel sind abgegeben bei: Hausmühl.

Wohnung (genaue Lage): v. I

D. B. 256

Inventar und Bewertung

Jeden Raum gesondert aufführen und mit Überschrift versehen (z. B. Schlafzimmer).
Nur zusammengehörige Sachen gemeinsam bewerten. — Kleinigkeiten als Sammelposten aufführen.

Lfd. Nr.	Stück	Gegenstand	Nähere Kennzeichnung	Bewertung in RM	Bemerkungen
		Wohnzimmer			
1	1	Kleiderschrank		5.—	
2	1	kl. Waschschrank		5.—	
3	1	runder Tisch		15.—	
4	5	Stühle		10.—	
5	1	Metallbettstelle kompl.			
		mit Betten		15.—	
6	1	Couch mit Betten		30.—	
7	1	Matratze u. Betten		5.—	
8	2	Blumentische		2.—	
9	3	Koffer		10.—	
10	1	Teppich	wertlos		
11	1	Beleuchtung		5.—	
12	1	Störse u. Übergardinen		10.—	
13	1	Kinderstuhl	wertlos		
14	1	Nachttischlampe	Porzellan	5.—	
15		Kleidung u. Wäsche		40.—	
		Korridor			
16	1	Flurgarderobe		1.—	
			zu übertragen Seitensumme: RM	150.—	

HWI 242a. Mat. 12060 a Din A 4 20000 4/43 J

The inventory of the contents of the Samuel family apartment, as com-
piled and evaluated by high court executor Wilhelm Vesper on May 20,
1943. See translation on the following pages. *(Brandenburgerisches Landeshauptarchiv)*

Lfd. Nr.	Stück	Gegenstand	Nähere Kennzeichnung	Bewertung in RM	Bemerkungen
—	—	Übertrag		153.-	
17	1	Reisekorb , Wanne und Waschgefäß		2.-	
		Küche			
18	1	Küchenschrank			
19	1	" kommode			
20	1	" tisch			
21		" stühle			
22	1	Handtuchhalter		40.-	
23	1	Stehleiter		1.-	
24	1	Kiste			
25	1	Waschständer		1.-	
26		Wäsche und Lumpen		15.-	
27		Porzellan u. Küchengeräte		3.-	
			Sa.	222.-	
		Kostenrechnung			
		Gebühr 5.00 RM		220.-	
		Porto 1.00 "		22,-	
		Schreibgeb. 2.0 "		198.-	
		Sa. 8.- RM			
		Bewertungssumme		220.-	
		Schätzkosten des OGV.		8.-	
			Sa.		
		Geschätzt auf 1 Blatt ,			
		Berlin , den 20 . Mai 1943			
		Gewissenhaft aufgenommen und bewertet			

zu übertragen Seitensumme: RM _____

Attention!

According to an agreement between the Executive Finance President, Berlin-Brandenburg, and the Executive Mayor of Berlin, reasonable moderate pricing based on prewar levels is to be applied in the evaluation of the items to be assessed.

Assessment sheet No. 1
(If there are several assessment sheets for a single dwelling, number them sequentially.)

Berlin: N 58   Street: Rhinowerstr.   No.: 11   Location: front
Previous renter or boarder: Cilly Sara Samuel
(Previous owner of the property)

Vermin-free! ~~Not vermin-free!~~   Key surrendered to: Waschinski
(Cross out the one that does not apply!)   Residence (exact location): Front, I

Inventory and Valuation

List contents of each room separately; give each section a title (e.g., bedroom).
Only pieces of a set should be assigned a joint value. List small items collectively.

Item No.	Pieces	Item	Distinguishing marks	Value in RM	Comments
		Living room			
1	1	Wardrobe		5.-	
2	1	Small linen chest		5.-	
3	1	Round table		15.-	
4	5	Chairs		10.-	
5	1	Metal bedstead, with bedding		15.-	
6	1	Couch with cushions		30.-	
7	1	Mattress and bedding		5.-	
8	2	Flower table		2.-	
9	3	Chests		10.-	
10	1	Carpets	worthless		
11	1	Lamps		5.-	
12	1	Curtains and drapes		10.-	
13	1	Child's chair	worthless		
14	1	Night table lamp	porcelain	5.-	
15		Clothing and linens		40.-	
		Hall			
16	1	Coat rack		1.-	

Total to be carried over to next page: RM   158.-

Item No.	Pieces	Item	Distinguishing marks	Value in RM	Comments
-	-	Carryover		158.-	
17	1	Basket, washbasin		2.-	
		and pitcher			
		Kitchen			
18	1	Kitchen cupboard			
19	1	" commode			
20	1	" table			
21	1	" chairs			
22	1	Towel rack		40.-	
23	1	Stepladder		1.-	
24	1	Chest			
25	1	Washstand		1.-	
26		Dishtowels and rags		15.-	
27		Dishes and utensils		3.-	
			Total	220.-	

Reckoning of costs
Fee   5.- RM
Transportation   1.- "
Paperwork   2.- "
        Total   8.- RM

Upper Court Executor   Assessment   220.-
                            Costs   8.-
                            Total   212.-

Berlin, 20 May 1943
Conscientiously recorded and evaluated
(Signature)
Upper Court Executor

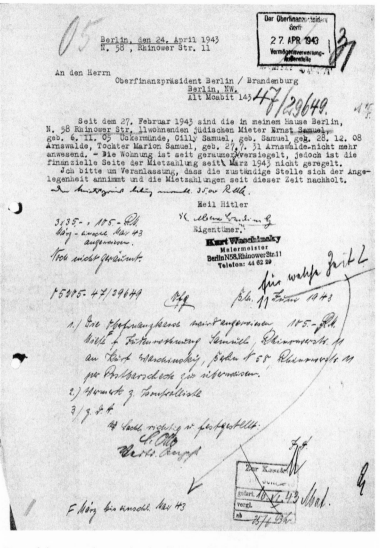

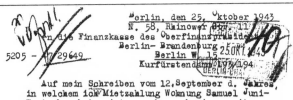

Auf mein Schreiben vom 12.September d. Jahres,
in welchem ich Mietzahlung Wohnung Samuel Juni-
September hat , ist nunmehr nach einem weiteren
Monat nur die Miete per Juni 43 im Betrage von 35,00
Rmk. geschickt worden und zwar am 13.9.43.
Da nun gleich der November vor der Tür steht , Werde
in Kürze Juli/November fällig, das sind 5 Monate
a 35,00 Rmk.= 175,00Rmk. Es wäre wohl nicht ver=
fehlt am Platze , da für jede Steuer pünktliche Zah-
lung gefordert wird , nunmehr auch um den pünktlicher
und besseren Mietzahlungsausgleich dieser Wohnung
nachzusuchen , ohne erst jedesmal von neuem darum
zu schreiben denn ohne Beschlagnahme wäre der Miet-
eingang ein normaler.

Ich hoffe also keine Fehlbitte getan zu
haben und zeichne
mit
Heil Hitler

I request that the responsible agency take up this matter and cover the rent for this period.

Heil Hitler
(Signature)
Property owner

According to the various stamps and other administrative markings that cover this letter, in June Waschinsky was allotted back rent "from March through May 1943." The second letter, dated October 25, 1943, says:

In response to my letter of 12 September of this year, in which I requested payment of the rent for the Samuel apartment, after yet another month I have only received the rent for June 1943, in the amount of 35 RM—and that on 13 September 1943.

As November is almost upon us, the rent for July through November is now due; that is, 5 months at 35 RM, or 175 RM. It should not be out of place, given that your office demands that property taxes be paid promptly, for me in turn to expect prompt recovery of the rent for this apartment without having to start the correspondence all over again each time from the beginning. Were it not for the confiscation, the rent would have been paid as usual.

I hope that I have not made an inappropriate request, and sign this with

Heil Hitler
(Signature)

(Brandenburgerisches Landeshauptarchiv)

Berliner Kraft - und Licht (Bewag) - Aktiengesellschaft
Reichsbetriebs-Nr. 5/0250/5003
Berlin NW.,7 Schiffbauerdamm 22
Fernruf: 42 00 11, Apparat 263
Postscheckkonto: Berlin 381 22

Meldung über evakuierte Juden

Rechnungsbüro — Rechnungsbüro Kopenhagenerstr.
Buchzeichen:
Aktenz. d. K/R:
Aktenz. d. Finanzamtes:

Unser früherer Abnehmer *Ernst Israel Samuel*
in der Anlage *Nr. 58, Rhinower Str. 11*
mit der jetzigen Anschrift *evakuiert*
hat eine **Rest-Schuld** für Stromverbrauch — aus dem E²-Geschäft — für Gebühren und Unkostenbeitrag RM *6.28*
Rest-Forderung aus der hinterlegten Stromsicherheit einschl. Zinsen
lt. untenstehender Aufstellung, die seit dem *5. 11. 38* fällig ist. (Rückseite beachten!)

Schuld f. Stromverbrauch lt. Rechng. v. *12.5.43*		RM *4.90*		
„ aus dem E²-Geschäft-lt.-Geschäfts-Nr.		RM		
„ für Gebühren und Unkostenbeitrag		RM	RM *4.90*	
Forderung aus der hinterlegten Stromsicherheit		RM *10.00*		
Zinsengutschrift bis *13.5.43*		RM *1.18*	RM *11.18*	

Es bleibt eine **Rest-Schuld** / Forderung auf dem Konto *3550/14/344* von RM *6.28*

Rechnungsbüro		K/R				K/FA	
ausgeschrieben	Dienststellenleiter	eingegangen	bearbeitet		weitergegeben	eingegangen	
13.5.43					*21.5.43*		
Datum Zeichen	Datum Zeichen	Datum	Datum Zeichen	Datum	Zeichen	Datum Zeichen	Datum Zeichen

---

Berlin Power and Light Corporation (Bewag)
Reich Firm No. 5/0250/5003
Berlin NW 7, Schiffbauerdamm 22
Long distance: 42 00 11, Ext. 263
Post office checking account:
Berlin 381 22

Report concerning evacuated Jews

Kopenhagenerstr. Accounting Office
Book:
File:
Finance Office File:

Our previous customer: *Ernst Israel Samuel*
Resident at: *Nr. 58, Rhinower Str. 11*
New address: *evacuated*
Has an outstanding ~~balance~~ credit for electricity to date, including interest, in the amount of *6.28 RM,* which has been due since *5 November 1938.*

Electricity usage reckoned from *12 May 1943* ....*RM 4.90*
Withdrawn from security deposit of ....*RM 10.00*
   plus interest to *13 May 1943* of ....*RM 1.18*..............................*RM 11.18*

There remains an outstanding ~~balance~~ credit for account *3550/14/344* of ....*RM 6.28*

Date Prepared	Prepared By	Received On	Processed	Transmitted	Sent Out

The May 1943 bill from the Berlin municipal electric company, on the special form that they had developed for payments due from residences of "evacuated Jews." See translation below. (*Brandenburgerisches Landeshauptarchiv*)

Der Oberfinanzpräsident
Berlin

Der Oberbürgermeister   Bln.-Schöneberg,d. 8.10.43.
der Reichshauptstadt Berlin   Hauptstr. 45
- Hauptwirtschaftsamt   Fernruf: 1 28 71 Anschl. 355

HWi 2 A

Zum Akt.Z. ...45/27-0-68...   ist Räumung
am ....2.7.9.43....

erfolgt.

An den

Herrn Oberfinanzpräsidenten   Im Auftrage
Berlin-Brandenburg   Rolde
-Vermögensverwertungsstelle-

B e r l i n   NW., 40
t-Moabit 143

In October 1943, the mayor of Berlin certified that the Samuel family's apartment had been emptied and could be rented once again. *(Brandenburgerisches Landeshauptarchiv)*

* * *

According to the train schedule for January 1943, trains for Auschwitz left Berlin-Moabit at 5:20 p.m. and arrived at their destination the next day at around 10:48 a.m.[60] Given what we know from survivors' accounts, the schedule in March was the same. The statistics kept by the Auschwitz camp commander show that Transport 33 from Berlin arrived with 1,886 people on board. These deportees did not leave the train at the now-infamous ramp at Birkenau. That 1.25-mile-long platform was only constructed fourteen months later, for the arrival of transports carrying Hungarian Jews.[61] In March 1943, the southwest area of the Oswiecim-Auschwitz train station—a siding on the main stretch of the Krakow-Prague-Vienna route—was designated the "Judenrampe." It was there that selections took place. Those deportees who were

Cilly Samuel's back wages, paid by Blaupunkt in May 1943 to the Berlin-Brandenburg tax office. The amount of 11.08 RM, which this form describes as "ceded to the Reich," would eventually be transferred to the government's main bank account and entered into the budget as "Reich income." *(Brandenburgerisches Landeshauptarchiv)*

not needed for work—usually the majority—were immediately and without any unnecessary effort sent straight to the gas chambers to be murdered. Those who were selected for work had their heads shaved, were tattooed with a number, and were clad in prisoner uniforms.

Of the 1,886 people on the train that brought Marion Samuel and her father to Auschwitz, 200 women received prisoner numbers 37296 to 37495, and 517 of the men received the numbers from 105571 to 106087. In other words, the SS commando in charge, which was usually led by a physician, sent a total of 717 people to be worked to death and the other 1,169 on their way to the gas chambers. At the conclusion of the selection, the head of labor deployment in the camp, SS-Obersturmführer Heinrich Schwarz, complained: "If the transports from Berlin continue to roll in carrying so many women and children and the elderly, I do not expect much as far as the needs of the labor force are concerned. Buna needs strong youths, above all." He was referring to the I. G. Farben factory in the Monowitz concentration camp, near Auschwitz, where thousands of prisoners were made to work and where the majority of them died.[62]

In addition to the deportees from Berlin, March 4, 1943, saw 1,000 men, women, and children from France arrive in Auschwitz. Of these, 881 were sent immediately to the gas chambers. Thus, on March 4, 1943, more than two thousand human beings were murdered in Auschwitz—all of them because they were Jews. Cilly Samuel had arrived two days before, on the thirty-first transport out of Berlin. In the case of that transport, 292 men and 385 women were selected for forced labor, while 1,161 were immediately murdered.[63]

It is possible that Cilly Samuel survived for a short period. We know for certain that the selection commando chose Ernst Samuel for forced labor: a note, "Died on May 4, 1943," is handwritten on his birth certificate in the registry at Ueckermünde. The note adds that the date of his death was determined by the "Arolsen Special Bureau, Auschwitz Department." The German town of Bad Arolsen is where the International Tracing Service of the Red Cross has been working since 1945 to clarify the fate of millions of people who were deported and murdered under the German regime, using tens of thousands of pages of deportation lists, card files, prisoner records, and documents from the camps.

In the concentration camp system of "annihilation through labor," Ernst Samuel survived for exactly sixty-one days. Marion

Samuel, however, was only a child, and a female child at that. The SS would not have considered her in any way fit for labor. On the morning of March 4, 1943, Marion Samuel was taken from her father and led to one of Auschwitz-Birkenau's two older gas chambers, Bunker I and Bunker II, which had been installed in former farmhouses. (The modern gassing and crematoria complex, which today represents the very concept of Auschwitz, was only opened a short time later.) According to the report of camp commandant Rudolph Höss, groups designated for gassing were sent "as soon as possible" on the 1.5-mile walk from the station platform to the bunkers. "Above all," Höss said, "it was important that the entire process of arrival and disrobing be carried out as peacefully as possible. No screams, no outbursts." Nevertheless, panic often broke out. It was met with violence, blows, and shouts; finally, with the rapid closing of the airtight bunker doors, the noise was stifled.[64] The gassing process has been described by eyewitnesses—but I shall refrain from quoting them here.

The first test of Auschwitz's new large crematoria, during which the corpses of forty-five men were incinerated in the presence of engineers from the Erfurt firm of Topf & Söhne, was carried out the day after Marion Samuel was murdered.[65] Therefore, the bodies of the more than two thousand Jews murdered on March 4, 1943, were burned instead in broad, somewhat secluded pits by the members of a special commando. Later, the graves were covered with soil. To this day, that area of Auschwitz-Birkenau remains, as a rule, free of bone fragments.

There is little more to be said about Marion Samuel's final days—as little as we know of her short life, marked as it was so early by state and societal violence and then destroyed.

The property declaration form for Marion Samuel that her father filled out has the word *son* jotted down in one corner by an official, with that word then crossed out and replaced with "daughter" in the same handwriting. We know, therefore, that Marion must have made a somewhat boyish first impression. And we can glean another little bit of visual information from Emilie Holz, who lived in Arnswalde until 1945: "Frau Samuel was a very lovely woman and her little daughter, Marion, had beautiful large brown eyes," she writes.[66]

In the end, though, the only person who can tell us something about what Marion felt is Hilma Krüger (née Kaul), the classmate who had spent a full year with Marion at the neighborhood public school in Berlin and who responded in 2003 to my appeal for information in the *Berliner Zeitung*. In the same letter where she first alerted me to the existence of a class photo, Hilma Krüger also described a conversation that took place in May 1938, just before Marion Samuel was required to leave that school:

I knew Marion Samuel, and to this day I cannot get her out of my mind. Again and again, when I read or hear something about the persecution of the Jews, I think of her. There is a reason why I cannot forget her. I used to walk with her to Frau Mollmann's class. She was a quiet, reserved girl, with a dark pageboy hairstyle and large almond eyes. I have only a vague memory of her face, because time has erased her appearance for me, but the memory of her eyes remains, and I know that I thought she was pretty. I was living then at Kopenhagener Strasse 66, and one day, at around six p.m., my mother sent me to the pharmacy on the corner of Rhinower and Gleim Strasse to pick up some medicine. On the way there, I saw Marion waiting outside her house. Because she had not been in school for a few days, I asked about her absence, and she replied that she had been sick. She was waiting for her mother. On the way back from the pharmacy I passed by her house again, and saw that she was still standing there. It must have been shortly before seven o'clock. We chatted about why her mother was so oddly late coming home. Suddenly Marion began to cry, and said that she was frightened. I was surprised, and then she said, "People go into a tunnel in a mountain, and along the way there is a great hole and they all fall in and disappear." I thought that she was acting a little crazy, and that this was a gruesome thing to say.

After that evening in May 1938, Hilma Krüger did not see Marion Samuel again. Marion had told her that she was a Jew, but children forget quickly, and Hilma herself went through several evacuations to the countryside during the war. "It was only in 1945," her letter continues, "now fourteen years old and once again in Berlin, that I saw a documentary film on Auschwitz and the other concentration camps. Suddenly, with horror, that day with Marion and her words about the tunnel rose up in my memory. She had probably overheard adults talking about things she could not fully comprehend, and then played out what she had heard in her child's fantasy. What terror she must have felt."[67]

Chapter 4

Portrait of a Persecuted Family

IN 1934, JENNY AND CARL SAMUEL, MARION'S MATERNAL grandparents, had given up their Arnswalde store under pressure from the town's Nazi sympathizers and moved to the Prussian city of Königsberg, some 250 miles away. They left the small town for much the same reason that Cilly and Ernst Samuel had moved to Berlin, seeking the anonymity of a large city. In small towns and villages, where everyone knew everyone else, the Nazis' domination of the local mood left Jews with little breathing space—especially when combined with the passivity of most of their former friends and classmates, their neighbors and their customers.

Helene, the eldest of Jenny and Carl's five children, was already living in Königsberg with her husband, Franz Pohl, who ran a small bicycle and radio shop. Arthur Samuel, the third of the Samuel siblings, also moved to Königsberg in May 1934. (The most likely reason for Arthur's move is that his wife, Ella, who came from a well-to-do family in nearby Tilsit, had good connections in the area and wanted to be closer to her relatives.) Martin Samuel, Jenny and Carl's second child, had moved to Berlin with his wife shortly before the birth of their daughter, Ruth, in 1926. The whereabouts at this time of Werner Samuel, Jenny and Carl's youngest child, who turned twenty in 1935, cannot be determined.

All three Samuel families in Königsberg lived near one another. Arthur, Ella, and their son lived in the old city at Holzwiesen Strasse 4; Helene and Franz Pohl lived with their children at Friedländer Torplatz 5; the elder Samuels lived at Kurfürstendamm 24. (Unlike the well-known glamorous avenue of the same name in Berlin, the Kurfürstendamm in Königsberg was a dead-end street in a rather modest neighborhood.) Carl and Jenny Samuel moved once more in 1939–40, perhaps to a "Judenhaus," a building exclusively for Jews; whatever the reason, by April 1940 their address was Georgstrasse 19.

The sole surviving group portrait of the Samuel family, shown to me by Erika Dünkel, Marion Samuel's cousin, was taken in Königsberg. The two copies of the photo that I saw—one in possession of Erika Dünkel, the other owned by Fred Samuel in New Jersey—tell some part of the family's story. Erika Dünkel's copy is scratched in the center of the image, testimony to the peregrinations and frequent handling of the photograph. During the final months of the war, Helene Pohl and her children hid on a farm, then fled and were driven from one place to another between the battle lines in East Prussia. Liberated eventually by Soviet troops, who both saved and abused them, they were not reunited with Franz Pohl until 1947. Throughout three years of uncertainty and frequent threats to their lives, Helene Pohl carried the family photograph stuck between copies of their papers, in a briefcase that she always kept nearby.

Fred Samuel's copy of the photograph represents the break in the family's history. He knew almost nothing of the people preserved there. Neither photograph carries any kind of inscription. Fred Samuel and Erika Dünkel are children in the picture, and had no knowledge of when the photograph was taken or what the occasion was for the family gathering.

It was nonetheless not hard to date the photograph. Erika, who sits on her father Franz's lap, looks a little over one year old, and Manfred (Fred Samuel)—in front, to the right of Marion—has to be at least four. If we note the celebratory summer clothing, and consider the grandparents' birthdays, then we can surmise that the photograph was taken on August 28, 1937: Jenny Samuel's sixtieth birthday, celebrated at Franz and Helene Pohl's home. Just over a year later, on November 17, 1938, Carl Samuel celebrated his seventieth birthday, but by this time—just after the Kristallnacht pogroms—a family gathering would have been no longer possible. Had the photograph been taken on Carl's birthday, Erika would have looked noticeably older, and the women would not have been wearing summer dresses.

The picture portrays the dignity of the Samuel family, and shows how they clung to the refuge of the tight family circle. They seem to be clinging as well to their middle-class status, yet the financial strain and the burden of isolation are visible in the faces of the adults. The life's work of the parents, the family business in Arnswalde, has been destroyed. Any hope for a small miracle has faded. Week by week, new repressions made the tortured search for an escape ever less realistic.

Franz Pohl sits at the left of the picture, the only Christian. In

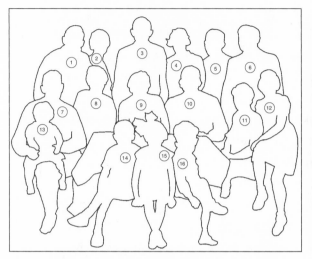

The last family photograph, taken in August 1937. (1) Arthur Samuel; (2) Ella Samuel; (3) Ernst Samuel; (4) Cilly Samuel; (5) Werner Samuel; (6) Martin Samuel; (7) Franz Pohl; (8) Helene Pohl; (9) Jenny Samuel; (10) Carl Samuel; (11) Hildegard Samuel; (12) Ruth Samuel; (13) Erika Pohl; (14) Wolfgang Pohl; (15) Marion Samuel; (16) Manfred (Fred) Moritz Samuel

Family tree of Marion Samuel's maternal relatives

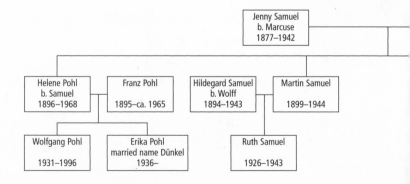

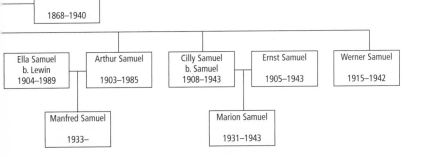

| Carl Samuel |
| 1868–1940 |

| Ella Samuel b. Lewin 1904–1989 | Arthur Samuel 1903–1985 | Cilly Samuel b. Samuel 1908–1943 | Ernst Samuel 1905–1943 | Werner Samuel 1915–1942 |

| Manfred Samuel 1933– | Marion Samuel 1931–1943 |

1933, he was suddenly deemed an "Aryan," thus considered better than the "non-Aryan" Jews. Again and again in the years to follow, the authorities tried to persuade him to divorce his wife, but he refused. Their marriage protected Helene and the children from deportation. After the promulgation of the Nuremberg racial laws in 1935, Franz and Helene's union was officially termed a "privileged mixed marriage": privileged so long as there were children, officially "half Jews," who were not being brought up Jewish.

On the left in the back row of the picture are Arthur Samuel and his wife, Ella. With an energy that is clearly evident in the photograph, they pursued emigration to the United States, saving themselves and their son. Next to them are Ernst, Cilly, Werner, and Martin Samuel. Martin stands behind his wife, Hildegard, while their daughter, Ruth, is perched on the arm of her chair. Little is known about the lives of Martin, Hildegard, and Ruth. If the reparations application submitted by Martin's surviving siblings, Helene and Arthur, is accurate, the resources of Martin's family were dwindling rapidly at the time the photograph was taken. In 1935, they had been forced to give up their spacious residence on a fashionable street in Berlin's Wilmersdorf borough and move into a much less desirable two-room apartment on Barbarossa Strasse in Berlin-Schöneberg.[68]

Arthur Samuel, who had taken over his parents' Arnswalde business in 1932 with great élan and new ideas, worked in Königsberg as a door-to-door salesman from 1934 until December 31, 1938, when the municipality withdrew his peddler's license. "I had to report to the employment office in Königsberg," he later wrote in a sketch of his experiences. "I was assigned to forced labor at a civil engineering firm, and I worked there until I emigrated on November 11, 1939. . . . I was no longer able to feed my family, and had to depend upon welfare."

*   *   *

It was impossible to find out very much about Werner Samuel—not even the exact date of his birth. According to Erika, his niece, her mother, Helene, was eighteen years old when he was born. That places his birth in 1915, when the Samuels were living in Arnswalde. "Werner visited us often," Leo Duschnitzki, a childhood playmate, remembered, somewhat vaguely; "he was a good friend, although somewhat reserved."[69] There is also one more telling piece of information. On April 14, 1940, Carl Samuel died of a lung infection at his Königsberg home at the age of seventy-one; his son Werner was

The memorial book for Carl Samuel. The title page reads "In Memoriam: Of my unforgettable Carl Isr. Samuel." The Hebrew inscription at the bottom is a traditional tombstone abbreviation of 1 Samuel 25:29: "May his soul be bound up in the bond of eternal life." (*Estate of Helene Pohl*)

the one who reported the death to the municipal registry. The death certificate says, "Entered on the evidence of the trainee Werner Israel Samuel, who lives at Neuendorf i. S."—that is, in Gut Neuendorf im Sande, today a section of the town of Fürstenwalde, which lies about thirty miles east of Berlin.

Neuendorf im Sande was home to Landwerk Neuendorf, a Jewish training camp that had been established there shortly before 1933. In this and in a number of similar camps, young Jews learned about farming, cattle breeding, and gardening to prepare themselves for the difficulties of building a new life in Palestine or elsewhere. The young men and women of these camps, readying themselves for emigration, were driven by various motivations and ideas about making a better world: socialism, national identification, a pioneer's desire for adventure. Part of the attraction, too, was a rejection of an ever more cerebral existence in favor of the romance of a simple life.

Key Jewish organizations saw the training of these young farmers as an important part of realizing nationalist ideals. Some of them spoke of transforming the nature of the Diaspora Jew, a sociological shift away from professional and mercantile minority occupations toward a life of manual labor. The young people called themselves trainees, as Werner Samuel had done when reporting his father's death. They dedicated themselves to learning Hebrew and saw themselves as Jews first and foremost. When the law required German Jews to wear the yellow star, the trainees at Landwerk Neuendorf held a "celebratory demonstration": they wore the "yellow badge with pride."

At first, the German government rarely intervened in the operation of these training camps. To a large extent, they remained autonomous, especially as long as the Zionist goal of settling in Palestine aligned with the general goal of the German leadership—to induce as many Jews as possible to emigrate. After the 1938 Kristall-nacht pogroms, however, these privately organized agricultural training centers were gradually transformed into comparatively mild labor camps. The political ideals upon which the camps were founded remained active through 1942–43, though, and while some camps were closed others continued to operate under Jewish leader-ship. Joel König, a trainee at Steckelsdorf (some forty-five miles west of Berlin), recalled that even after the beginning of the war, the camp remained "a peaceful enclave": "there, we were allowed to live."

The work at the camps, which had once been voluntary, now proceeded on the basis of an agreement with the government. Af-ter the war started, trainees from Landwerk Neuendorf were sent to work on the Oderbruch highway, in the lumber industry, in pri-vate gardens, or on local farms. In a way, the camps actually bene-fited from the increased state intervention, because concrete participation in such training programs protected Jewish men from arbitrary transfers to concentration camps. For some among the twenty-five thousand Jewish men arrested after the pogroms, proof of a place in a training camp could be sufficient to bring about their release.

Through at least 1939 and 1940, Werner Samuel was among the more than 250 trainees at Gut Neuendorf. Like almost all the young men and women suffering under persecution, he likely dreamed of a new life of self-determination, in Palestine or elsewhere.[70]

A glance at the family photograph is enough to see that the Samuels were relentlessly slipping out of their middle-class status. Self-confident men and women who had always supported them-selves, they were now welfare recipients. The photo shows them helpless, disappointed, and defenseless—threatened by a growing, subjectively incomprehensible persecution absurd in its details. The celebrants at this party have been thrown back on their own resources and are barely in a position to help one another in weathering their shared circumstances. Eight of the sixteen men, women, and children in the picture were murdered only a few years later. That they would die had not yet been decided by the German leadership in the summer of 1937, but the photo provides a premonition. Victor Klemperer, the Jewish-German academic who by this time had been rendered "stateless," recalls 1937 in his diary: "the terrible standstill of time, the hopeless vegetating."[71]

The most prominent subject of conversation at the family gathering in Königsberg must have been the question of emigration. Where to? With what funds? With what risks? And what would happen to those left behind? Werner Samuel was already preparing for emigration. Helene Pohl, who trusted that her Christian husband would continue to protect her and her children, most probably offered to take care of Carl and Jenny.

For Ernst, Cilly, and Marion Samuel, as well as for Martin, Hildegard, and Ruth, the conversation must have been fraught with uncertainty and fear. It is reasonable to surmise that they did not have the money required to emigrate. How often emigration was discussed, with how much anxiety regarding the future, is perhaps revealed in the oppressive, strangely vivid and portentous nightmare that Marion would share with her classmate nine months later. "People go into a tunnel in a mountain, and along the way there is a great hole and they all fall in and disappear."

The idea of emigration gained the most momentum with Arthur and Ella Samuel. Arthur Samuel had lost his livelihood in Arnswalde, and in Königsberg had had to carry on under very difficult conditions. More than anyone else in the extended family, his wife, Ella, had both money and connections. With a certain level of confidence, the adults discussed a plan for emigration in stages. Because Ella's sister Lena and her husband, Richard, had lived in the United States for a number of years, Arthur, Ella, and Manfred would go first, and then bring the others over after them.

Just before the 1938 pogrom, Arthur and Ella received a guarantee of support from Isidor A. Kalver, a movie theater owner in Fort Wayne, Indiana. Kalver obligated himself to the United States of America to provide support for the family of Arthur Samuel and for his mother-in-law and a sister-in-law. He declared himself prepared—and this was the prerequisite without which a visa could not be issued—to provide the impoverished refugees with the minimum means necessary in case of emergency, including food, shelter, clothing, and medical treatment. The guarantor had to agree to provide this support for an unlimited period of time, and regardless of the amount of funds required: "I unqualifiedly guarantee the support of the aliens so long as they remain in the United States, should such aliens require such support at any time to prevent them from becoming a public charge."

The family was able to emigrate at the last minute. Arthur was the first to leave for New York, in November 1939; Ella, her mother, and the six-year-old Manfred followed in January. Ella's brother-in-law Richard wired over the necessary $500—equivalent to about $7,000 in today's money. The Samuels were not allowed to have direct control of the funds; instead, the Reichsbank in Tilsit transferred $104.50 for the cost of passage directly to the Holland-America Line in Rotterdam. The authorities in East Prussia also demanded a "non-refundable deposit" of 122 RM to cover the "Reichsfluchtsteuer," the tax for "fleeing the Reich." Still, the

Telegram from Ella Samuel to her relatives in New York: "In possession of all visas, departure possible only if Holland Line is booked."

departure finally took place, and today lead crystal glasses brought from Germany stand in a cabinet in Fred Samuel's home.

In the United States, Arthur and Ella Samuel could at first barely keep their household above water. Arthur worked as a door-to-door salesman, peddling carpets and draperies. Ella, meanwhile, worked in a factory, trying to earn enough money to quickly pay back the cost of the passage. After the war, Arthur and his sister Helene, who was then living in the East German town of Greifswald, corresponded weekly, and in 1962 they finally saw each other for a few days in Karlsbad. This reunion after twenty-three years was made possible by reparations paid on behalf of their murdered brother Martin. Arthur and Helene could not, however, seek reparations on behalf of Ernst Samuel's family, because he had not owned anything of significant worth. Reparations were paid only for the loss of material possessions, not for the murder of a human being. Arthur Samuel died in New York in 1985.[72]

In 1948, as part of her application for recognition as a victim of fascism in Soviet-occupied Greifswald, Helene Pohl wrote an account of her life under the Nazis:

> I, Helene Pohl, b. Samuel, was born on November 30, 1896, in Werben, Pyritz, Pomerania, the daughter of Carl Samuel, a Jewish businessman, and his Jewish wife, Jenny, b. Marcuse. From the ages of six to fourteen, I attended school in Arnswalde, Neumark, where my parents had moved shortly after I turned one year old. After I left school, I worked in my parents' business until my marriage.
>
> On July 5, 1922, I married the businessman Franz Pohl and moved to Königsberg, Prussia. On August 19, 1931, I gave birth to a son, and on July 1, 1936, my daughter was born. My husband had a bicycle and radio shop in Königsberg, and I often helped out there. After 1933 we suffered much under the Nazi regime, and very soon I had to cease working in my husband's shop. The Nazi persecution went so far that in the later years, I did not even dare enter the shop.
>
> My husband was sent to a camp on November 22, 1944, by order of the Gestapo, and I was robbed of all protection. I could not remain with my children in Königsberg, because a large action against the Jews had been planned for that city, and I sought to avoid it. I had gotten wind of a plan to take the children away from Jewish parents and to deport us. I announced my intention to travel to Berlin. In order to avoid another such disaster, though, I did not go there. Instead, I took my children to a trusted acquaintance, the farmer Fritz Glandien in Mansfeld (Samland), who had proved himself a true

N.V. NEDERLANDSCH-AMERIKAANSCHE STOOMVAART-MAATSCHAPPIJ

HOLLAND-AMERIKA LIJN

(HOLLAND-AMERIKA LINIE)

GENERALVERTRETUNG
HOLLÄNDISCHES VERKEHRSBÜRO G.m.b.H.
BUDAPESTER STRASSE 42
(AN DER GEDÄCHTNISKIRCHE)

MITGLIED NR. 3421
DER FACHGRUPPE „REISEVERMITTLUNG"

TELEGRAMME
HOLLANDLINIEN BERLIN
FERNSPRECHER
SAMMEL-NR. 25 33 55
POSTSCHECK-KONTO
BERLIN NW 7, Nr. 16957
BANK-KONTO
DEUTSCHE BANK
Dep.-K. Joachimstaler Str. 4
Berlin-Charlottenburg 2

DIE BEFÖRDERUNG DER PASSAGIERE
SCHIEHT IN UEBEREINSTIMMUNG MIT DEN
BDINGUNGEN DER UEBERFAHRTSVERTRÄGE

BERLIN W 50, DEN 2. Dezember 19

St./Li.

HAUPTBÜRO:
ROTTERDAM

FILIALEN IN:
AMSTERDAM
BOULOGNE s/MER
GENF
HAMBURG
KÖLN
LONDON
MÜNCHEN
PARIS
PRAG
STUTTGART
WARSCHAU
WIEN
ZÜRICH

NEW YORK
BALTIMORE
BOSTON
CHICAGO
CLEVELAND
LOS ANGELES
MONTREAL
PHILADELPHIA
SAN FRANCISCO
ST. LOUIS

VERTRETER
IN ALLEN STÄDTEN
EUROPAS
UND AMERIKAS

Frau
Ella S a m u e l
per Adr. Lewin

T i l s i t
Deutschestr. 67

Betrifft: Ihre Passage nach New York.

Hierdurch teilen wir Ihnen mit, dass ein weiterer Passage-
betrag in Höhe von $ 104.00 laut erhaltenem Avis der
Holland-Amerika Linie, Rotterdam für Sie und Ihren Sohn
für die Passage nach New York eingegangen ist.

Wir bitten um umgehende Mitteilung, wann Sie Ihre Über-
fahrt nach New York antreten. Im Augenblick ist nur noch
Platz in der III.Klasse auf dem Dampfer "Statendam" am
29. Dezember 1939.
Falls Sie mit dem Dampfer "Statendam" fahren wollen, bitten
wir um Überweisung von RM. 10.- Telegrammkosten, um die
Plätze für Sie anfragen zu können.

Hochachtungsvoll

Holländisches Verkehrsbüro G.m.b.H.

friend and an anti-fascist. Glandien and his family took us in, hid us out of sight of the Nazis, and cared for us—without any prior notice and without ration cards—until the arrival of the Russians.

As is well-known to all, full Jews such as myself suffered much under the enmity of the Nazis. My mother and my siblings were taken with their entire families and sent to the East. I have not heard from them again. My paternal inheritance, a store in Arnswalde, Neumark, at Markt 9, was confiscated from us by the Nazis and destroyed. We got only the minimum necessary amount of food, which is all that was allowed to Jews; all we had were little special disbursements, because we were not allowed to enter many of the stores. We underwent frequent house searches. That our existence hung by a slender thread, and that we often feared for our lives and had to hide, is known worldwide and does not need extra mention.

My children, who are "half Jews," experienced endless hostility from their schoolmates (who were, of course, Hitler Youth). They also suffered hostility from the teachers, and their performance was constantly undervalued.

Greifswald, March 16, 1948—Helene Pohl.[73]

OPPOSITE: A letter to Ella Samuel from the Dutch travel bureau. The text reads:

Concerning your passage to New York:
According to the Holland-America Line, the amount of $104.50 has been received on your and your son's behalf for travel to New York.
We request by return mail the date on which you wish to begin your voyage. At the moment, there remain only 3rd Class berths on the ship *Statendam* on 29 December 1939.
If you wish to travel on the *Statendam*, we request that you wire over 10 RM in telegraph costs so that we can hold the places for you.
Respectfully,
For the Dutch Travel Bureau, Inc.,
(Signature)

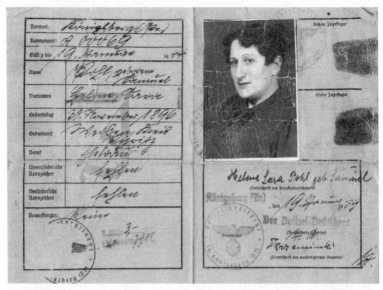

Helene Pohl's Jewish identity card, issued to her in Königsberg on January 19, 1939. Besides her name, occupation, identification number, and registered place of residence, the card includes prints of both index fingers. It is signed "Helene Sara Pohl."

Hidden behind this matter-of-fact report are experiences that Helene Pohl did not wish to describe in greater detail. As her mother and brother were being deported, she enrolled her "half-Jewish" daughter, Erika, in the local public school. Shortly before, an Evangelical pastor had baptized the girl and her brother, Wolfgang, in their home. At school, however, as "half Jews," the two children—each one the only "half Jew" in his or her class—had to sit apart and alone on a bench, isolated from the other children. Both were struck with a stick by the teacher more often than the other, "Aryan" children.

After the arrest of her mother, Helene Pohl left Königsberg with her children and went into hiding. She gave the police a forwarding address with one "Fräulein E. Zander" at Brabanter Strasse

Erika Pohl's ceremonial photograph on her first day of school, Königsberg, 1942. She is holding a *Schultüte*, the candy-filled paper cone that German children traditionally receive on the occasion.

17 in Berlin-Wilmersdorf. Helene had lived there with a Jewish woman named Selma Michaelis, and both Zander and Michaelis were her friends. She told Erika and Wolfgang that if they got separated from her, they were to try to make it to that address. In November 1944, Helene and her children went into hiding with Glandien in the village of Mansfeld, about seven miles from Königsberg. An attempt to travel to Berlin by train failed because the great Weichsel bridge near Dirschau had been destroyed in an explosion. At the end of January 1945, Helene, Wolfgang, and Erika tried to leave East Prussia on the ship *Wilhelm Gustloff*, but got no farther than the harbor at Pillau. Missing the boat turned out to be fortunate, for it was torpedoed off the coast of Pomerania and sank with 5,200 refugees aboard.

In her report, Helene Pohl identified the farmer Glandien as "a true friend and an anti-fascist." With those words, she erected a small, silent monument to him. As the Russian army rolled through Germany, Glandien, his wife, his daughter, and a small grandchild were rounded up by Russian soldiers along with other civilians from the village and summarily shot. Helene Pohl and her children were marched with other refugees east toward the town of Gumbinnen, and later driven on foot back from there to the now-destroyed Königsberg. The victorious army had burned many houses in the city. Absolute chaos, death, and rape were the order of the day.

Now Helene Pohl and her children were considered Germans. She fought this designation with every means. Again and again she found Jewish officers who were willing to help her. Franz Pohl, meanwhile, searched for his family with the help of the International Red Cross, and eventually met with success. After an indescribable odyssey—emaciated, beaten down, and often at the limit of their strength—Helene, Wolfgang, and Erika Pohl finally arrived in the

MINISTRY OF INTERNAL AFFAIRS—USSR
ADMINISTRATION OF MINISTRY OF INTERNAL AFFAIRS OF KALININGRAD REGION

2 April 1947   Number 8   City of Kaliningrad

PASS

Issued: 14.4.47

Last Name ___Pohl___
First Name ___Helene___
Year and place of birth ___1896 / Pyritz Pomerania___

Permitting him [sic] unimpeded passage from the Kaliningrad region to the Soviet zone of occupation of Germany.

Route: KALININGRAD—POLAND—KÜSTRIN
Accompanied by children:
Pohl Wolfgang born 1931   Pohl Erika born 1936
Pass valid for 3 months from date of issue.

HEAD OF ADMINISTRATION OF MINISTRY OF INTERNAL AFFAIRS
OF KALININGRAD REGION
MAJOR-GENERAL   (TROFIMOV)

A pass issued to Helene Pohl in April 1947, permitting her and her children to travel out of Soviet-occupied East Prussia. After months of wandering through Poland, forced labor, and many difficulties in crossing the border, Helene Pohl was finally able to return to what would later become East Germany with the help of a Jewish officer.

Bernburg reception camp in the Soviet zone of occupation on June 27, 1947. The family was reunited in Greifswald, which had largely escaped destruction. There, as victims of fascism, Franz and Helene Pohl were awarded a small schnapps and spirits store.

After all they had gone through, though, the marriage broke down. Franz Pohl moved to the Western zone. Helene took over the business, and became active in the Association of Victims of the Nazi Regime. After her retirement, she worked as a volunteer in the Greifswald welfare department. She died in 1968.

On the morning of June 24, 1942, Jenny Samuel and her son Werner reported as ordered to a former indoor riding arena near Königsberg's north train station. They had been notified of their impending deportation in advance, in writing, and told that they would be allowed to take only sixty-five pounds of baggage with them. In all, approximately 470 men, women, and children bearing the yellow star made their way to the train station, obeying an order for their deportation to an unknown destination "in the East."

Jenny Samuel was one of the oldest to be deported from Königsberg that day. Two months later she would have turned sixty-five, and been deported on a smaller transport to the "old-age ghetto" at Theresienstadt instead of being placed on the only eastern transport to leave Königsberg. Erika, who was almost six years old at the time, remembers how she and her mother, Helene, accompanied Jenny to the station, pulling her baggage behind them in a small wagon. They had to part when they came to a blockade. As an eyewitness, the then fourteen-year-old Michael Wieck, later described the scene:

> Several hundred people had been ordered to report to the assembly point at the same time. Each one had been sent directions and

Jenny and Werner Samuel at Carl Samuel's grave in the
Jewish cemetery in Königsberg, 1940

regulations. They were allowed to take only sixty-five pounds of
baggage, but everyone had more. It was incredible to see what people had dared to take with them. One could feel each person's shock
and dismay. The deportation action was comprehensive and spared
no one. The entire morning, the Jews marched through the streets

carrying their belongings. Some of them had to pause every few steps to catch their breath, others had small handcarts. The expressions on their faces were empty, resigned, but also anxious.

Wieck's report goes on to say: "These innocent, ostracized people passed through the streets, and with only a few exceptions their former fellow citizens, patients, customers, friends, or neighbors stood idly by and watched, or turned away. Some looked on with bitter feelings, with knowledge of a terrible injustice and of their own powerlessness. Nevertheless, those who had the opportunity to do so all profited from the goods, houses, apartments, furnishings, books, and jobs the Jews left behind."

When they arrived in the riding arena, the deportees were required to conclude the process of their own dispossession. The officials carried out this last "paper assault" with extreme accuracy. "Everything was conducted correctly," Wieck recalls; "amicably businesslike, even contentedly so."

Then the whole group had to walk from the assembly point to the Königsberg freight depot. According to the special schedule, their train was to leave at 10:34 p.m. By around seven p.m. it was ready to be loaded. "Suddenly, there was an entire company of uniformed personnel, and the guards were no long neutral or correct." The deportees boarded the third-class cars that were waiting for them. Their baggage was loaded into a separate car at the end of the train; that car was then uncoupled and left standing in the depot.[74]

On June 15, in preparation for the trip, the Reichsbahn (Germany's national railway authority) had designated the train as "Da 40." "Da" was the abbreviation for all the special trains that were used for deporting Jews. Exactly what it meant is not documented, but perhaps it can be inferred by analogy: a "Dg" train was a train for freight (*Güter*), so perhaps a "Da" was a train for resettlement (*Aussiedlung*). The scheduling directive sent by the Reichsbahn to Königsberg describes the train's destination and its client: "A special train for the conveyance of settlers from Königsberg in north Prussia via the Königsberg Vbf [marshaling yard]—Bialystok to Wolkowysk, destination Minsk. Ordered by the Reich Main Security Office, Berlin." In its special instructions, the railway administration noted: "Information about the itinerary and schedule is not to be given out to non-participants, including the passengers of the train." The passengers would leave the passenger cars at Wolkowysk, on the southeastern edge of the Königsberg region, and board freight cars. On the same evening of June 24, 1942, a train with a few wagons departed from the city of Allenstein, carrying between 80 and 120 Jews; one can assume that the two trains were coupled at the station in Korschen.[75]

On Friday, June 26, 1942, the deportees arrived on schedule in the Minsk freight depot. From there, they traveled into the forest at Maly Trostinez. In the forest the deportees were either shot or—as was more often the case—suffocated with exhaust fumes in a truck functioning as a mobile gas chamber. In his report on the action, an SS-Unterscharführer named Arlt wrote: "The work of the remaining men here in Minsk remains much the same. The Jewish transports arrive at regular intervals, and we attend to them. On June 18–19 we were once again occupied with digging pits in the settlement area. . . . On June 26, the expected Jewish transport from the Reich arrived."

This "expected transport" contained the Jews from Königsberg and Allenstein. "Attended to" was the SS officer's euphemism for their murder, and "settlement area" referred to the mass graves for several thousand men, women, and children in the Maly Trostinez

Deutsche Reichsbahn · Königsberg(Pr), den 15.6.1942
Reichsbahndirektion Königsberg(Pr)
33 Bfp 9 Bfsv

Nur für den Dienstgebrauch!

Fahrplananordnung Nr. 46

für einen Sonderzug zur Beförderung von Aussiedlern

von Königsberg(Pr) Nord über Königsberg Vbf - Bialystok
nach Wolkowysk, Ziel Minsk. Besteller: Reichssicherheitshaupt-
amt Berlin.
Gültig am 24. auf 25. Juni 1942.

A. Fahrpläne siehe folgende Seiten.

B. Besondere Anordnungen.

a) Die Bekanntgabe der Sonderzüge an die beteiligten Bedien-
steten hat nach FV § 66 (7) zu erfolgen.

b) Umbaustellen, Langsamfahrsignale und Fahrbeschränkungen
gemäß A s F V und La sind sorgfältig zu beachten.

c) Durchfahrt der Sonderzug Bahnhöfe, auf denen alle Regel-
züge halten, so sind die Geschwindigkeitsbeschränkungen
innerhalb dieser Bahnhöfe zu beachten. (FV § 70, 2)

) Die Überholung von Zügen und das Abwarten von Kreuzungen
und Überholungen sind am Schlusse des Fahrplans in der
Reihenfolge der Bahnhöfe angegeben. Die Zugfolge nicht
genannter Züge regeln die Fahrdienstleiter.

e) In Spalte 9 sind die Fahrzeiten im Abschnitten in einer
Summe angegeben. Die einzelnen kürzesten Fahrzeiten können dem Buchfahrplan der betr. Strecke entnommen werden.
regelt Ozl Lokdienst.

) Lok- und Personalstellung
Bei Schwierigkeiten in der Lokstellung ist
teil M30 - Fernsprecher 1908 - anzurufen.

g) Diese Fahrplananordnung geht den Dienststellen unmittel-
bar zu. Der Eingang ist dem vorgesetzten Amt zu bestä-
tigen.

27874

164

Orders issued by the railway office for the June 24, 1942, "Special Train for the Conveyance of Emigrants," on which Jenny and Werner Samuel were deported from Königsberg to the death camp at Maly Trostinez. "When passing through rail stations at which the regular trains have been halted for the special train, obey speed limits within the station," the instructions note. "Permission has been given to overtake trains, as well as to wait at crossings and on bypass tracks at the series of stations at the end of this schedule." The train's itinerary, given at the top of this form, is described on page 105. (Hilberg, Sonderzüge)

The package receipt from Auschwitz, stamped RETURN/HOLD FOR NEW ADDRESS—Helene Pohl's de facto notification of the death of her brother Martin Samuel

forest. There, on June 26, 1942, Jenny and Werner Samuel were killed.[76]

Some eight months later, on February 19, 1943, Martin, Hildegard, and Ruth Samuel were deported to Auschwitz. Until her deportation, Ruth, then a teenager, had been forced to work at Siemens Kabelwerk, in Berlin-Gartenfelde, for fourteen marks net per week.[77] Martin Samuel's family traveled together from Berlin to Auschwitz in Transport 29. It was the same journey that Cilly, Ernst, and Marion Samuel would make on Transports 31 and 33 less than three weeks later.

Ruth and Hildegard died in Auschwitz the day of their arrival or shortly thereafter. For Martin Samuel, there are a few signs of life for some time beyond his deportation. He was registered in Auschwitz as prisoner number 103915 on February 20, 1943. On April 22, his name was entered into the record book of Block 21, the hospital block. It shows up again on August 5, 1943, in the main camp records, with a note that Martin had undergone an X-ray examination.

Helene Pohl regularly sent packages to her brother in Auschwitz.[78] The last one was returned to her by the "Postzensurstelle K.L. Auschwitz" (Post Censor's Office, Concentration Camp Auschwitz) on February 29, 1944, stamped RETURN/HOLD FOR NEW ADDRESS. Helene knew immediately that this was, in effect, Martin's death certificate. She placed the Auschwitz-stamped package receipt in an envelope with the most important family documents.

Afterword

Walther Seinsch,
cofounder of the Remembrance Foundation
and the Marion Samuel Prize

In empty spaces,
As though caught in a spiderweb of wire,
The piles of shoes grow, the shoes of corpses:
Small shoes, children's shoes, men's shoes,
The shoes of little girls.
—*The first stanza of a poem composed by a twelve-year-old girl at the end of 1943 in the Majdanek concentration camp*

MARION SAMUEL'S SHOES DISAPPEARED INTO SUCH A pile—soon after she was sent to the gas chamber.

On his own initiative and with great persistence, Götz Aly investigated the life of this child and her family, and we offer him heartfelt thanks. We feel ourselves challenged to speak of the names and stories of thousands of other human beings who suffered a similar fate. This book will help us to do that: it shows how, even under unfavorable conditions, the fate of those who seem nameless and unknowable can, indeed, be recovered. The postwar generations are obliged to illuminate the unmistakable individuality of those who had to die simply because of their "race." Aly's often incomplete yet vivid sketch of the life of Marion Samuel instructs us how to do so.

We must research, document, and remember—especially because the liars, the relativizers, and those who want to simply stop thinking about the events all continue in their work. Creative and heartless, they seek to bend the facts: to forget, displace, varnish over, escape from the responsibility of speaking the truth. Ultimately, not speaking the truth means ignoring the victims, including Marion Samuel.

Thirty-five years after the Second World War, when a new generation of historians began employing more focused methods of investigation, their path was not always easy. If their research turned out to be all too accurate, if they named people or institutions that had until then presented themselves as blameless, then their concrete discoveries detailing German crimes of the war years were contested, denied, and defamed.

Christian Streit's investigation of the fate of Soviet prisoners of war, published in 1978 as *Keine Kameraden*, is one example. Streit established that of the approximately 3.3 million Soviet prisoners of war in the custody of the Wehrmacht, tens of thousands were shot while millions were deliberately starved and later perished at inhuman hard labor. Upon the book's publication, historians, generals, alleged witnesses, and experts with mountains of inaccurate and falsified numbers attacked Streit with hatred and derision. In 1989, when Soviet archives were opened and outside historians could for the first time examine the documents directly, Streit's controversial research was confirmed. The number of victims, however, required correction: it was even higher than the minimum determined by Streit.

But even undisputed facts cannot halt the tendency toward whitewashing in recent German histories. For instance, Heinz Trettner, the former inspector general of the federal German army, claimed in the *Bonner Generalanzeiger* on March 11, 1997, that "contrary to what the re-education propaganda maintains, it can be demonstrated today that the war against the Soviet Union was, first and foremost, a preventative war, begun by force of necessity and with a heavy heart. From the first day, inhuman behavior was introduced by overheated Soviet soldiers, who murdered German prisoners of war."

Others have sought to find exoneration by decrying what they call the disproportionate guilt and shame heaped on Germans. They take issue with the fact that crimes committed against Germans or carried out by other people are too often not recognized. The deceivers and relativizers also promote the argument that all this talk about Nazi crimes prevents the recovery of German identity: they fret that the consequence for Germans of constantly humbling themselves abroad is the stoop of the shamed, or a hatred of their own land.

This is nonsense. Precisely because I have concerned myself with the history of the twentieth century, including its darkest days, I look upon Germany as my true country and see myself as a German patriot. My sympathies are with the thousands of Germans engaged in political, economic, and social causes; with those who work against nuclear arms or help the handicapped or children disabled by war. I cheer on German soccer teams when they play abroad. I am proud of German philosophers, musicians, painters, poets, and scientists. I would not even exchange our politicians, for, in the end, Germany is a state based on human rights and with an exemplary constitution.

My feelings about my country and my fellow citizens would not be possible were I to diminish or relativize German crimes. As the political scientist Gesine Schwan put it, "Do we lose our dignity when we remember, or do we win back our dignity precisely through the act of remembering?"

For the sake of true memory, there can be no taboos or prohibitions on thought. Yes, we must speak of the expulsion of ethnic Germans after World War II; of the labor Germans were forced to perform; of the firebombing of German cities; of the failed peace of Versailles. But the great number of human beings who fell victim to political violence must still be remembered. For the Samuel family, that happens in this book. The Remembrance Foundation hopes, in this way, to advance the memorialization of individuals.

Scholarship free of ideology and corruption is an indispensable foundation for our task. But even more important, it appears, is a readiness not to reduce the victims to nameless corpses at Auschwitz. The dead were persecuted as members of a collective: as "Jews," "subhumans," "racially worthless." If we wish to preserve our dignity, we must restore to them their individuality. They were young and old, poor and rich, men and women, children full of dreams and hopes—like Marion Samuel, a child with a ribbon in her hair.

Notes

1. Götz Aly, "Von den tragenden Volkskräften isoliert. Rudolf Schottlaender oder die Verbreitung von Licht," in Aly, *Rasse und Klasse. Nachforschungen zum deutschen Wesen* (Frankfurt am Main, 2003), pp. 216–29.

2. *Gedenkbuch für die Opfer der Verfolgung der Juden unter der nationalsozialistischen Gewaltherrschaft in Deutschland 1933–1945,* Bundesarchiv-Koblenz/International Tracing Service Arolsen (Koblenz, 1986), p. 1289.

3. *Gedenkbuch Berlins der jüdischen Opfer des Nationalsozialismus.* Freie Universität Berlin, Zentralinstitut für Geschichte (Berlin, 1995).

4. Götz Aly, "Bürgerliche Klarheit," *Berliner Zeitung,* April 21, 1999.

5. Bundesarchiv-Berlin, ZSg 138/302, p. 99.

6. Ibid., R 1501 (Reichsinnenministerium).

7. Expropriation files, Brandenburgerisches Landeshauptarchiv-Potsdam, Rep. 36A Oberfinanzpräsident Berlin-Brandenburg (II), 33198, 33199, 29649.

8. *Berliner Zeitung,* February 7, 2003.

9. Ibid., March 17, 2003.

10. Götz Aly, "Das unbekannte Mädchen. Marion Samuel: 1931 in Arnswalde geboren, in Berlin zur Schule gegangen, 1943 in Auschwitz ermordet," *Berliner Zeitung,* May 10–11, 2003.

11. Jessica Goodman, "Portrait from the Past: Fair Lawn Man Learns the Fate of Relatives Caught in the Shoah," *Jewish Community News* (Jewish Federations of North Jersey and Greater Clifton-Passaic), August 15, 2003; reprinted in *New Jersey Jewish Standard,* August 15, 2003.

12. Margin notes on the birth certificate (192/1905) of Ernst Samuel, "Married No. 91 1929 Arnswalde," Registration Office, Ueckermünde.
13. Property declaration submitted by Cilly Samuel on February 28, 1943, in Berlin (see note 7).
14. List of residents of the city of Arnswalde, October 1, 1924. (I am grateful to Wolfgang Palm for this information.)
15. Supplemental birth certificate for Carl Samuel, issued on January 11, 1880, by the Royal Prussian District Court Stargard in Pomerania; from the papers of Helene Pohl, born Samuel: "Mein Lebenslauf, Helene Pohl (b. Samuel), March 16, 1948, Greifswald," Landesarchive Greifswald, Rep. 200/9.2.1, No. 2099; draft life story, written by Arthur Samuel in New York (n.d.), in the papers of Arthur Samuel, Fred M. Samuel, Fair Lawn, New Jersey.
16. The report supplements the article "Marion-Samuel-Preis" by Wolfgang Palm, *Heimatgruss-Rundbrief* 249 (2000), p. 35, and 255 (2001), p. 26. This article on the creation of the Marion Samuel Prize is based on an article that I wrote on the occasion of the awarding of the first prize to Raul Hilberg (see note 4).
17. Wolfgang Palm, "Drei Photos aus dem jüdischen Leben von Arnswalde," *Heimatgruss-Rundbrief* 253 (2001), p. 36. Because Ruth Duschnitzki (married name Bartal) is pictured in this photograph, Palm "on this occasion" published her letter of November 11, 1993, to Dr. Erdmann Kreusch.
18. Fritz Mörke and Wolfgang Palm, "Jüdische Familien in Arnswalde," *Heimatgruss-Rundbrief* 223 (1993), pp. 41–44; 224 (1994), pp. 10–11; 225 (1994), pp. 25–27 (hereafter Mörke/Palm).
19. Alfred Jachmann was born in Arnswalde in 1927. He was the only member of his family to survive their deportation to Auschwitz. After the war, he lived in West Berlin and later in Frankfurt am Main, where he died in 2002. Alfred Jachmann, "Lernen Sie aus den Fehlern der Grosseltern," at http://www.wetteraukreis.de/pressestelle2002/themen/dezernat-a/jachmann.htm (accessed January 2003).
20. Wolfgang Palm, supplement to the article "Marion-Samuel-Preis," *Heimatgruss-Rundbrief* 255 (2001), p. 26.
21. Papers of Arthur Samuel; Mörke/Palm, p. 11.
22. The August 20, 1935, meeting is cited in Raul Hilberg, *The Destruction of the European Jews* (New Haven, 2003), p. 35.
23. Wolfgang Palm, "Die 'Stiftung Erinnerung' und der Marion-Samuel-Preis," *Heimatgruss-Rundbrief* 249 (2000), p. 35.
24. "Erlass des Führers und Reichskanzlers über die Verwertung des eingezogenen Vermögens von Reichsfeinden, May 29, 1941," Reichsgesetzblatt I/1941, p. 303; details can be found in Bundesarchiv-Berlin R 1501/1838 (Reichsinnenministerium).
25. Inge Kameke, "Erinnerungen an meine Mitschülerin Gerda Jachmann (geb. 30.8.1925, umgebracht im KZ Auschwitz)," *Heimatgruss-Rundbrief* 222 (1993), p. 45. Gerda Jachmann was deported from Berlin to Auschwitz on March 2, 1943.
26. L. Duschnitzki to G. Aly on January 27, 2003.
27. R. Bartal in conversation with G. Aly on January 22, 2004.
28. A. Jachmann (see note 19).
29. Mörke/Palm, p. 45.
30. Ibid., p. 41; for the results of the census of May 17, 1939, see http://www.literad.de/regional/arnswalde.html (accessed December 2002), p. 1.

31. Helmut Eschwege, *Die Synagoge in der deutschen Geschichte* (Dresden, 1980), p. 183.

32. Mörke/Palm, p. 41; W. Palm to G. Aly on January 24, 2003. Salewsky's watercolor of the Jewish cemetery in Arnswalde was published as the cover of *HR* 250 (2000).

33. Alfred Jachmann interview with Susann Heenen-Wolff, in Heenen-Wolff, *Im Haus des Henkers. Gespräche in Deutschland* (Frankfurt am Main, 1992), pp. 224–39.

34. Frank Wagner, *Auf den Spuren der jüdischen Mitbürger in Ueckermünde* (Ueckermünde, 2001). Declaration of Hildegard Cohn, b. Samuel (sister of Ernst Samuel) from October 10, 1957, Landesentschädigungsamts-Berlin, 251805; Heinz Grosskopf, *Ueckermünde. Beiträge zur Geschichte der Stadt und der Region* (Ueckermünde, 2002), pp. 38, 70, 106.

35. Birth certificate of Ernst Samuel, Standesamt-Ueckermünde.

36. Heinrich von Treitschke, "Unsere Aussichten," in *Deutsche Kämpfe. Schriften zur Tagespolitik.* Neue Folge (Leipzig, 1896), p. 23.

37. Wagner, "Jüdische Mitbürger," p. 9 (see note 34).

38. Ibid., pp. 22*ff.*

39. Landesentschädigungsamt-Berlin, 260414, 70456, 251805; birth certificates of Margarethe and Ernst Samuel, Standesamt-Ueckermünde; supplemental cards from the census of 1939, Bundesarchiv-Berlin, R 1509; e-mail from Shaul Ferrero (Yad Vashem) to G. Aly on January 15, 2003.

40. For more on the deportation from Stettin, see Else Rosengeld and Gertrud Luckner, eds., *Lebenszeichen aus Piaski. Briefe Deportierter aus dem Distrikt Lublin 1941–1943* (Munich, 1968), pp. 76, 87; Götz Aly, "Endlösung," in *Völkerverschiebung und der Mord an den europäischen Juden* (Frankfurt am Main, 1995), pp. 85, 97–98.

41. Mörke/Palm, p. 25.

42. Helene Pohl, "Mein Lebenslauf " (see note 15).

43. Expropriation files (see note 7).

44. Ibid. On the form filled out by high court executor Vesper on June 12, 1943, one can find the exact location of the apartment.

45. During school hours in the fall of 1946, the school blew up because a Soviet soldier guarding the building accidentally ignited a munitions storage in the cellar—a gruesome accident that cost many lives.

46. The card for Marion Samuel in the card file for Jewish students, Bundesarchiv-Berlin ZSg 138/302, Bl. 99–100.

47. This passage is based on the excellent essays by Birgit Kirchhöfer, "Für und wider eine neue Schule. Die jüdische Schule in der Rykestrasse," in Bernt Roder, ed., *Schule zwischen gestern und morgen. Beiträge zur Schulgeschichte von [Berlin] Prenzlauer Berg* (Berlin, 2002), pp. 372–94; ibid., " 'Das Gefühl der Geborgenheit.' Die jüdische Schule in der Rykestr. 53," in *Leben mit der Erinnerung. Jüdische Geschichte in Prenzlauer Berg.* Prenzlauer Berg Museum (Berlin, 1997), pp. 296–315.

48. "Mitteilung des Reichsministeriums für Wissenschaft, Erziehung und Volksbildungs an die Unterrichtsverwaltungen der Länder und Reichsgaue, July 7, 1942," Brandenburgisches Landeshauptarchiv, Rep. 2AII Gen 1260, Bl. 16. (I am grateful to Birgit Kirchhöfer for this document.)

49. Personnel books, Werk Berlin-Marienfelde, DaimlerChrysler AG, Konzernarchiv Stuttgart.

50. Expropriations files (see note 7).

51. Camilla Neumann, "Erlebnisbericht aus der Hitlerzeit," Part 1. Leo Baeck Institute, New York, JMM 59. (I am grateful to Wolf Gruner for this information.)

52. See Wolf Gruner's groundbreaking essay, "Die Fabrikaktion und die Ereignisse in der Berliner Rosenstrasse," in *Jahrbuch für Antisemitismusforschung* 11 (2003), pp. 137–77.

53. C. Neumann, Part 2 (see note 51).

54. Message from the finance president of Westfalen in Münster to local finance offices, December 8, 1941. In Wolfgang Dressen, ed., *Betrifft: "Aktion 3." Deutsche verwerten jüdische Nachbarn. Dokumente zur Arisierung, ausgewählt und kommentiert* (Berlin, 1998), pp. 77*ff.*

55. Ibid; Frank Bajohr, *"Arisierung" in Hamburg. Die Verdrängung der jüdischen Unternehmen 1933–1945* (Hamburg, 1997), pp. 331–38. The memories of secondhand store clerk Lothar Berfelde are to be found in Martin Friedenberger, Klaus-Dieter Gössel, and Eberhard Schönknecht, eds., *Die Reichsfinanzverwaltung im Nationalsozialismus* (Berlin, 2002), pp. 82–83; the quotation there is from Dorothea Kolland, ed., *Zehn Brüder waren wir gewesen . . . Spuren jüdischen Lebens in [Berlin-]Neukölln* (Berlin, 1988).

56. Personnel books, Werk Berlin-Marienfelde (see note 49).

57. All details of the actual conditions of the deportation are based on the property declarations and the appended expropriation documentation (see note 7), and on the corresponding deportation lists for Transports 31, 32, and 33. "Transport von Berliner Juden nach Auschwitz," Brandenburgerisches Landeshauptarchiv-Potsdam, Rep. 36A/55142/43/44.

58. C. Neumann, Part 2 (see note 51).

59. G. Aly, "Endlösung," pp. 380*ff.*

60. Raul Hilberg, *Sonderzüge nach Auschwitz* (Mainz, 1981), pp. 41–42, 212.

61. Christian Gerlach and Götz Aly, *Das letzte Kapitel. Realpolitik, Ideologie und der Mord an den ungarischen Juden 1944/45* (Stuttgart/Munich, 2002), pp. 255, 274.

62. Danuta Czech, *Kalendarium der Ereignisse im Konzentrationslager Auschwitz-Birkenau 1939–1945* (Reinbeck bei Hamburg, 1989), p. 430.

63. I am grateful to Jochen August for the more accurate numbers that he sent me in response to my request to the Archiv der Gedenkstätte Auschwitz. Czech, p. 430.

64. Martin Broszat, ed., *Kommandant in Auschwitz. Autobiographische Aufzeichnungen des Rudolf Höss* (Stuttgart, 1963), pp. 127*ff.*

65. Czech, p. 432; Jean-Claude Pressac, *Die Krematorien von Auschwitz. Die Technik des Massenmordes* (Munich, 1994).

66. Palm (see note 20).

67. H. Krüger to G. Aly on February 8, 2003. The documentary film that she refers to is *Die Todesmühlen* (The Death Mills), released in fall 1945, written and directed by Hanus Burger and edited by Billy Wilder. (I am grateful to Gisela Eimermacher for this information.)

68. Expropriation files for Martin Samuel, Brandenburgisches Landeshauptarchiv Rep. 36A, Oberfinanzpräsident Berlin-Brandenburg 33215.

69. L. Duschnitzki to G. Aly on January 19, 2004.

70. Wolf Gruner, *Der geschlossene Arbeitseinsatz deutscher Juden. Zur Zwangsarbeit als Element der Verfolgung 1938 bis 1943* (Berlin, 1997); Eliyahu Kutti Salinger, *"Nächstes Jahr im Kibbutz." Die jüdisch-chaluzische Jugendbewegung in Deutschland zwischen 1933 und 1943* (Paderborn, 1998), about Neuendorf, pp. 188*ff.*; Werner T. Angress, *Between Fear and Hope: Jewish Youth in the Third Reich* (New York, 1988). (I am grateful to Susanne Heim and Wolf Gruner for the important information about this material.)

71. Victor Klemperer, *I Will Bear Witness: A Diary of the Nazi Years, 1933–1941* (New York, 1999), p. 243.

72. Papers of Arthur Samuel (see note 15). The letters from his siblings have not been preserved.

73. Helene Pohl, "Mein Lebenslauf" (see note 15).

74. Michael Wieck, *Zeugnis vom Untergang Königsbergs. Ein "Geltungsjude" berichtet* (Heidelberg, 1989), pp. 30–35.

75. For the most important details about the deportation from Königsberg I am grateful to Alfred Gottwaldt in Berlin, who kindly allowed me a glimpse into his unpublished manuscript titled "Die Deportation der Juden aus Ostpreussen während der Jahre 1942/43 und ein Bericht des Allensteiner Artztes Dr. Heinrich Wolfheim von 1947."

76. For information about Maly Trostinez, see Hans Safrian, *Die Eichmann-Männer* (Vienna-Zurich, 1993), pp. 183–89; Christian Gerlach, *Kalkulierte Morde. Die deutsche Wirtschafts- und Vernichtungspolitik in Weissrussland 1941 bis 1944* (Hamburg, 1999), pp. 747–74; Hilberg, *Sonderzüge*, pp. 164–66.

77. Property declaration of Ruth "Sara" Samuel from February 6, 1943, Brandenburgisches Landeshauptarchiv Rep. 36A/33215.

78. Archives of the Auschwitz State Museum, "Buch des Häftlingskrankenhaus, Block 21, Chirgurie, Bd. 2, Bl. 72 (D-AuI-5/2, Inventarnr. 71080); "Röntgenbuch des Häftlingskrankenhaus des K.L. Auschwitz (Stammlager), Bd. 15, Bl. 55 (D-AuI-5/15, Inventarnr. 5034). (I am grateful to Jochen August for referring me to these documents in the archive and for showing me that Marion Samuel's name was crossed off the list for Transport 32.)

Bibliography

Götz Aly. *"Final Solution": Nazi Population Policy and the Murder of the European Jews.* Translated from the German by Belinda Cooper and Allison Brown. London and New York: Arnold, 1999.

Götz Aly and Karl Heinz Roth. *Die restlose Erfassung. Volkszählen, Identifizieren, Aussondern im Nationalsozialismus.* Frankfurt am Main: Fischer Taschenbuch Verlag, 2000.

Werner T. Angress. *Between Fear and Hope: Jewish Youth in the Third Reich.* Translated by Werner T. Angress and Christine Granger. New York: Columbia University Press, 1988.

Frank Bajohr. "Aryanisation" in *Hamburg: The Economic Exclusion of Jews and the Confiscation of Their Property in Nazi Germany.* New York: Berghahn Books, 2002.

Else Behrend-Rosenfeld and Gertrud Luckner, eds. *Lebenszeichen aus Piaski: Briefe Deportierter aus dem Distrikt Lublin, 1940–1943.* Afterword by Albrecht Goes. Munich: Deutscher Taschenbuch Verlag, 1968.

Danuta Czech. *Kalendarium der Ereignisse im Konzentrationslager Auschwitz-Birkenau 1939–1945.* Reinbek bei Hamburg: Rowohlt, 1989.

Das Daimler-Benz-Buch. Ein Rüstungskonzern im "Tausendjährigen Reich." Nördlingen, 1987.

Wolfgang Dressen, ed. *Betrifft: "Aktion 3": Deutsche verwerten jüdische Nachbarn: Dokumente zur Arisierung.* Berlin: Aufbau-Verlag, 1998.

Helmut Eschwege. *Die Synagoge in der deutschen Geschichte: eine Dokumentation*. Dresden: VEB Verlag der Kunst, 1988.

Martin Friedenberger, Klaus-Dieter Gössel, and Eberhard Schönknecht, eds. *Die Reichsfinanzverwaltung im Nationalsozialismus: Darstellung und Dokumente*. Bremen: Edition Temmen, 2002.

Gedenkbuch Berlins der jüdischen Opfer des Nationalsozialismus. "Ihre Namen mögen nie vergessen werden!" Freie Universität–Berlin. Zentralinstitut für Geschichte: Berlin, 1995.

Gedenkbuch: Opfer der Verfolgung der Juden unter der nationalsozialistischen Gewaltherrschaft in Deutschland, 1933–1945. Bundesarchiv-Koblenz and the International Tracing Service, Arolsen. Frankfurt am Main: J. Weisbecker, 1986.

Christian Gerlach. *Kalkulierte Morde: Die deutsche Wirtschafts- und Vernichtungspolitik in Weissrussland 1941 bis 1944*. Hamburg: Hamburger Edition, 2000.

Christian Gerlach and Götz Aly. *Das letzte Kapitel: Realpolitik, Ideologie und der Mord an den ungarischen Juden 1944–1945*. Stuttgart: Deutsche Verlags-Anstalt, 2002.

Alfred Gottwaldt. "Die Deportation der Juden aus Ostpreussen während der Jahre 1942/43 und ein Bericht der Allensteiner Artztes Dr. Heinrich Wolfheim von 1947." In *Gedächtnisschrift für Helge Grabitz und Festschrift zum 75. Geburtstag von Professor Dr. Wolfgang Scheffler*. Berlin: Haus der Wannsee-Konferenz, 2004.

Wolf Gruner. "Die Fabrikaktion und die Ereignisse in der Berliner-Rosenstrasse." *Jahrbuch für Antisemitismusforschung* 11 (2003): 137–77.

———. "Der geschlossene Arbeitseinstaz deutscher Juden. Zur Zwangsarbeit als Element der Verfolgung 1938 bis 1943." Berlin, 1997.

Susann Heenen-Wolff, ed., *Im Haus des Henkers. Gespräche in Deutschland*. Dvorah: Frankfurt am Main, 1992.

Raul Hilberg. *Sonderzüge nach Auschwitz*. Frankfurt am Main: Ullstein, 1987.

———. *The Destruction of the European Jews*. 3 vols. New Haven: Yale University Press, 2003.

Rudolf Höss. *Commandant of Auschwitz: The Autobiography of Rudolf Hoess*. Translated by Constantine FitzGibbon. London: Phoenix Press, 2000.

Birgit Kirchhöfer. "Für und wider eine neue Schule. Die jüdische Schule in der Rykestrasse." In Bernt Roder, ed., *Schule zwischen gestern und morgen. Beiträge zur Schulegeschichte von [Berlin-]Prenzlauer Berg*. Berlin: Schneider Verlag Hohengehren, 2002.

Victor Klemperer. *I Will Bear Witness: A Diary of the Nazi Years*. Translated by Martin Chalmers. 2 vols. New York: Modern Library, 1999.

Joel König [Ezra BenGershôm]. *David: The Testimony of a Holocaust Survivor*. Translated by J. A. Underwood. New York: Oswald Wolff Books, 1988.

Dorothea Kolland, ed. *Zehn Brüder waren wir gewesen . . . Spuren jüdischen Lebens in Berlin-Neukölln*. Gesellschaft für ein Jüdisches Museum in Berlin, Bezirksamt Neukölln von Berlin, Abt. Volksbildung/Kunstamt, Emil-Fischer-Heimatsmuseum. Berlin: Edition Hentrich, 1988.

Primo Levi. *If This Is a Man*. Translated by Stuart Woolf, with an introduction by Paul Bailey and an afterword by the author. London: Abacus, 1987.

————. *Survival in Auschwitz: The Nazi Assault on Humanity*. Translated by Stuart Woolf. New York: Collier Books, 1959.

————. *The Drowned and the Saved*. Translated by Raymond Rosenthal. New York: Summit Books, 1988.

Dieter Pohl. *Holocaust: Die Ursachen, das Geschehen, die Folgen*. Freiburg: Herder, 2000.

Prenzlauer Berg Museum. *Leben mit der Erinnerung. Jüdische Geschichte in Prenzlauer Berg*. Berlin, 1997.

Jean-Claude Pressac. *Die Krematorien von Auschwitz: Die Technik des Massenmordes*. Translated [from the French] by Eliane Hagedorn and Barbara Reitz. Introduction by Ernst Piper. Munich: Piper, 1995.

Hans Safrian. *Die Eichmann-Männer*. Vienna: Europaverlag, 1993.

————. *Eichmann und seine Gehilfen*. Frankfurt am Main: Fischer Taschenbuch Verlag, 1995.

Eliyahu Kutti Salinger. *"Nächstes Jahr im Kibbutz." Die jüdische-chaluzische Jugendbewegung in Deutschland zwischen 1933 und 1943*. Paderborn: KoWAG Universität Paderborn, 1998.

Gesine Schwan. *Politik und Schuld: Die zerstörerische Macht des Schweigens*. Frankfurt am Main: Fischer Taschenbuch, 1997.

Roman Vishniac. *A Vanished World*. Foreword by Elie Wiesel. New York: Farrar, Straus and Giroux, 1983.

Frank Wagner. *Auf den Spuren der jüdischen Mitbürger in Ueckermünde*. Stadt Ueckermünde: Heimatbund "August Bartelt" Ueckermünde, 2001.

Michael Wieck. *Zeugnis vom Untergang Königsbergs. Ein "Geltungsjude" berichtet*. Foreword by Siegfried Lenz. Heidelberg: L. Schneider, 1989.

About the Author

One of the most respected historians of the Third Reich and the Holocaust, GÖTZ ALY is the author of *Hitler's Beneficiaries* and *Architects of Annihilation*, among other books. He has been a Visiting Fellow at the United States Holocaust Memorial Museum in Washington, D.C., and currently teaches at the Free University of Berlin.